Lies My Momma Told Me

Renna Jo Damon

ISBN: 9798650143109
LCCN: 2020923431

Cover Illustration: Jim Guevara
Interior Format: Phyllis Clemmons
Editing: Phyllis Clemmons

The Herriott Sisters

Jeannie, Jo, Lois, Myra

DEDICATIONS

I dedicate this book to every name mentioned within these pages. Without them, the book would not exist.

ACKNOWLEDGEMENT

I would like to acknowledge all of my family for making this book possible through their encouragement and to my Momma, Betty Mae Herriott, for being herself and enriching my life.

January 17, 1926 to July 7, 1984.

I'll see you in a few years on the other side.

TABLE OF CONTENTS

Aunt Jo's Hobby

*H*ow can I explain my Aunt Jo? She was a character. I am her namesake and proud to be, but I am not sure I understand her even now. She died in ninety-one, leaving six dogs and a houseful of cats for her husband to deal with. Her house was a maze of boxes stacked to the rafters with left-overs from her treasure hunting days.

I think some of the boxes were actually holding up the rafters. Her hobby was redesigning costume jewelry. She had boxes and tins full of broken brooches and earrings and necklaces in every corner of her home.

She had things that a collector would die for. She had about a hundred metal lunch boxes. Everything from the "Wizard of Oz" to "The Jetsons" was depicted on the tin boxes. Some still had the original thermal bottles in them.

These she used for her rhinestones. A different color in each bottle made the job of rebuilding a brooch easier. Aunt Jo had a box of doll arms that stayed in the same corner of her living room for twenty years! This may not strike you as weird. But having no two arms alike, that's weird!

Optimism All The Way

*G*randma was eighty-three years old and still very active. Her favorite pastime was her beautiful flowers. My Aunt Jo went to the store and also ran other errands, leaving Grandma home alone.

A dog or something had dug a hole in the garden unknown to my grandma. She tripped in it and fell. Her arm landed on a rock, and she twisted her ankle.

Undaunted, she dragged herself to the house. There were several steps she could not manage so she crawled under the porch.

When Aunt Jo got home she put the groceries away and thinking Grandma was napping, stayed quiet and fell asleep herself for a while. Aunt Jo woke to Grandma's shouts of, "Help me!"

Aunt Jo began searching for Grandma and found her quickly. Grandma said, "What took you so long? It was hot out here." Aunt

Jo replied, "Well, at least you were in the shade."

Aunt Jo, took her to the hospital. After an x-ray was taken, it was discovered that Grandma had a broken arm. For the first time in her life, she experienced a broken bone.

When Grandma got home, she was not unhappy as one would expect. Her joy came from knowing that even with a busted wing, she could still attend to her garden.

Romance Goes Out The Window

*W*eirdness, seems to run in our family. It even crossed over to spouses. For instance, my husband is not one you might call crazy, like my Aunt Jo. But he is sometimes very weird.

Oh, he was romantic enough in the beginning of our relationship. But as the years slipped by, (sigh)…

On our twelfth anniversary we went out to dinner and a movie. This was in 1979 before videos. We had seen an early movie and were headed home.

I mentioned that I was not ready to go home. I had hoped he would feel romantic and we'd go where all the lovers go on a Saturday night.

We were on a dark road on our way home with only the full moon and our headlights to show the way.

I said, "Look honey, it's a full moon!"
Don stopped the car, stuck his head out the
window and howled like a wolf. He pulled
his head back inside the car and we
continued on. I am sometimes amazed at the
difference between a man's thinking and a
woman's thinking. My hint to invoke
romance made Don think of comedy instead.

The only thing that saved Don that year
was the dozen roses he had delivered the
next day. Our life together does not read like
a romance novel, but instead, it was more
like a comic book.

The Summer Of Rebuilt Toys

*O*nce, I asked my Aunt Jo for a piece of gum. She began digging into her purse to find one. She pulled out a hammer, some fishing lures, a coping saw, a pair of pliers, a half dozen mirrors and sixteen combs.

Now, one might think she put the combs in her purse because she had forgotten she had one already, not so. You see, Aunt Jo always had combs so she could style the hair of any doll or doll's head she might find. If she could not make the hair presentable, she'd leave it at the dump.

Aunt Jo would also shop at other thrift stores. She had a knack for finding the best bargains. Aunt Jo would load up a box of broken toys. She would offer a dollar or two for the unusable merchandise, knowing she could make good toys by cannibalizing the parts.
She had a huge collection of doll arms, legs, and heads. She would use the torso of one doll, the legs of another, and the head of yet another to create a lovely new doll.

The summer I turned seventeen, I spent helping Aunt Jo make toys.

This method of rebuilding toys was not limited to dolls. Aunt Jo also dealt in bikes, trikes, and wagons.

That summer we made thirty-two tricycles and about fifty dolls. We put them away for the Christmas sale.

Aunt Jo had a three foot tall walking doll she was trying to find an arm for. She was having no luck. She never found a suitable arm for the doll.

Shortly after Christmas that year, Aunt Jo closed up shop forever, so that she could spend more time taking care of Grandma.

She kept that one armed doll standing in the corner of her bedroom for the next twenty years.

I Am My Own Cousin

I am my own cousin. My daddy's parents were first cousins. Their mothers were sisters.

In the early nineteen-hundreds families settled on the same plot of land, reared their children, and raised their crops together.

There might not have been another unrelated family within several day's journey.

They had a tendency of marrying those who were available.

Travel was not as easy or common back then, so when it came time to choose a bride the pickings were slim.

Claude and Willie were first cousins and their children were second cousins. The children of the second cousins were third cousins.

This means that my grandparents are my cousins because they are cousins to each other. My dad is my cousin as well as cousin to his own two sisters.

My sisters are my cousins because they are the children of my cousin and I am my cousin by being the child of my cousin.

One Good Turn

I had a date, but because I was still very young, Momma said I couldn't go unless my sister went too. She was three years younger but she had a date as well.

Her date was a friend of my date. We were going to the zoo and the amusement park.

After walking on and on in the heat, looking at all the smelly old animals we'd seen many times before, we each got a big hamburger and a soda.

The hamburgers were the delicious, greasy kind that teased you into more than one.

Lois' date ate two burgers. The rest of us only ate one. Lois didn't finish hers, but offered it to her companion instead.
He ate that, too. We went to the amusement section of Forest Park and rode some of the rides. We rode the tilt-a-whirl, the carousel, the scrambler, and the roller coaster like contraption called 'The Mad House.'

Our last ride before going home was the Ferris Wheel. On the fourth revolution, Lois' friend began to feel queasy and turned a lovely shade of chartreuse.

He lost his hamburger over the side of the car we were in and in, as well as in the car, on my sister's shoes, and lap.

He wretched for what seemed like forever as kids and adults alike, on the ground, scrambled out of the line of fire.

The four of us screamed for the operator of the ride to stop the ride. He yelled up to us that he couldn't stop the ride, as it was on a timer and had to make ten revolutions before it would stop. That boy spewed so much, I think he threw up every ounce of baby formula he'd ever drank.

We Got A Piano

My Aunt Dorothy was in need of some repairs on her house. There was some dead shrubbery to be cut and hauled away and the house needed a new roof.

Daddy offered to do the job. He agreed to do it without pay as a favor to his beloved aunt.

Daddy did a very good job and Aunt Dorothy insisted he take something in payment, despite the previous agreement.

Aunt Dorothy struck a deal to give Daddy her old Piano for us kids. He agreed and bought it home that day.

In the winter we always closed off the dining room and living room to conserve heating fuel.

The piano was put in the living room for lack of a better place to put it as it was quite large. We were not allowed to go into the part of the house because it was so cold. Momma was afraid we would get sick.

Spring came and it was time to open up the entire house. Finally we could discover our talent on that old piano.

Actually, all we did was bang on it. None of us had a lick of 'natural born talent.'

The blessing came when Daddy got transferred to the night shift on his job. He had to sleep days so we could not 'play' the piano during the day. We lost interest in the instrument due to sheer abstinence.

Daddy sold the piano shortly before the family moved again.

Boo-Ji

*W*hen my sister, Betty Jean was small, she would not go to sleep on any schedule. This made life difficult for our Momma. Because she was expecting Lois at the time and was less than exuberant in the first trimester.

Every time we'd go to visit Grandma, Betty Jean would fall asleep before we got home.

Daddy got the idea of taking Jeannie, (as I have always called her) for a ride until she fell asleep.

The old model A Ford Daddy had back then was about as noisy as a car can get with grinds and rattles coming from every moving part. Daddy marveled that anyone could sleep through such racket.

Daddy began to talk to my sister. He was saying over and over, "Betty Jean's a pretty thing." Each time he said it she would laugh. Then she uttered her first phrase, "Boo-Ji za pert chang"

Kiss Your Elbow

*M*omma's have a thing about passing on things they endured in their childhood to their unsuspecting daughters. I would love to ring the neck of the sadist who authored this evil little lie.

We were three little girls. Daddy referred to me as his almost son. I was more like him than my sisters were. I was short, stocky, left handed and inquisitive. He used me as his helper on many occasions when he had a project to do around the house. His frequent referral to me as "Daddy's boy," made me want to be a boy. I wanted so much to please him.

I don't remember how it fit into the conversation that day, but Momma told me and my sisters that she had heard that if we kissed our own elbow, we would turn into a boy.

I nearly ripped my arm out of its socket trying to be the boy I thought my daddy wanted.

Years later Momma and Daddy had another child. Daddy finally got his fourth daughter. I say finally because she was the end of the line for them. Brothers are nice I suppose, but I would not trade my sisters for a brother.

The Day My Slip Slipped

Can-can slips were a necessary addition to the wardrobe of every adolescent girl in the 1950's. My sister and I, each had one. They were a gift from our Aunt Jo. She was really the one who kept us in style. We never wore just one. We took turns wearing both of the slips. We may as well have been wearing a tutu under our dresses. The hem of our skirts were a full six inches further out than any of the other girl's.

It happened that it was my turn to wear the can-cans. I wore them both under my favorite skirt. The poodle skirt was all the rage and every well-dressed girl in her teens had one.

Jeannie was a bit larger in the waist than I was, so I had to secure the slips with a safety pin.

While at school, just as I was called on to do a math problem on the board, the safety pin popped open and my can-can slips hit the floor. It was a full two minutes before the laughter subsided. I took the slips and the teacher's stapler to the restroom, where I stapled a pleat in the can-cans at the elastic waistband.

I used about twenty staples, but it kept my can-cans in place for the rest of the day.

Mashed Tomatoes

My cousins, Ernest and Erby have always been my favorite cousins. We never were around any of the others much. Most of the time, they were nice to us. But once in a while they would turn on us.

One such occasion was when my cousin's step-dad had made a very nice garden one year.

It had produced so many pearl tomatoes that he had placed a box of them on the front porch for the neighbor to take and enjoy, if they wanted them.

The neighbors had taken all they wanted and the rest of the tomatoes had gotten quite ripe. My cousin suggested we play a game which required me to be led blind-folded around the yard.

I was to guess where I was and who was leading me. There was to be no talking in order not to give this information away. Silently he led me to the front porch where my other cousin had lined up twenty ripe tomatoes in the path of my bare feet. That was the only mean trick I ever remember my cousins playing on me.

Of all my cousins, they are the best as they apologized for the prank and were really nice to me from that point on. Boy cousins and girl cousins are rarely good friends.

The Sparrow Sandwich

One childhood friend, Tommy got a gun for Christmas. He was ten years old at the time. His instructions were to be careful and not to point the gun at any living creature he did not intend to eat. It was thought that a live target was not easy to hit, so they were safe…wrong!

To teach Tommy a valuable lesson he had to pluck, clean, and cook the sparrow he killed. He had to eat a sparrow sandwich! He never took aim on so much as a grasshopper again.

Once again, the animals were safe, both beast and fowl.

Tommy practiced shooting by placing pennies in an anthill and shooting them out. He may have killed a few ants, but who cares?

He'll Only Do It Once

A friend of my momma's had a little boy 12 months old. Momma went to borrow some flour so she could bake a cake.

Hen Momma got to her friend's house she was busy mopping her kitchen floor. Her little boy was sitting on the table playing with his toys. He seemed to be quite content.

Momma was appalled at the sight of that baby on the table.

Momma asked the woman, "Aren't you afraid he might fall off?"

"No," she replied, "Besides, if he does, he'll only do it once."

Momma Catches A Dogfish

*M*omma was about eight months pregnant with my baby sister when we went to Padre Island for a vacation.

My sisters and I enjoyed the sand and the cool water, but Momma would not venture out into the water past her knees. She preferred to sit on a beach on the pier and fish.

She was catching mostly eels and an occasional crab, but not much else. Nothing she could size up for a frying pan would come near her line.

Momma was the only one on the beach that day who was not dressed in swimming apparel. It was obvious to all that she would be delivering soon.

Daddy had advanced to the end of the pier in hopes he would be able to get at the big ones and also to avoid having to stop every ten minutes to rebait Momma's hook.

All of a sudden, Momma let out a blood curdling scream. Everyone on the pier, turned to look at her.

Daddy heard her even from the distance he was. He came running to see what was upsetting her. Momma was hysterical.

People thought she had gone into labor and offered to carry her to the car. Momma was in a panic because she had hooked a dogfish. (A dogfish was about the ugliest fish God ever created). All Momma could say was "Get him off. Get him off. I don't want him. Get him off!"

Daddy reached into his tackle box and got his four-blade pocket knife and honored her request. Momma was so relieved that she slept during the entire return trip back to San Antonio.

I Hate Sports

I was not a very good student in grade school. My best subject was music and my best grade was a C. I simply did not apply myself to my studies. I had such an introverted personality that it interfered with my being involved in class participation.

My fifth grade teacher thought I was a deaf mute for the first week I was in her class. I enjoyed certain subjects and my field of interest did not include any sports.

I hated softball. I was victimized in dodge ball. I did not understand volleyball or soccer.

I did like Jump rope, for about all of ten minutes. Then I was ready to sit down to a rollicking game of jacks.

The crippled boy in my class and I became good friends. Because he could not play and I didn't want to. When our class was assigned to read Victor Hugo's classic, *Hunchback of Notre Dame,* I refused to read it because I thought it was about football!

Aunt Jo Loses Her Keys

*I*f one is weird acting and wealthy, he or she is eccentric. If one is weird and poor, he or she is just plain crazy. My Aunt Jo was crazy. One year, she decided she could make a lot of money in the re-sale business. She rented a small shop in the North end of San Antonio where she had lived for almost all of my life.

She could go to the city dump, and for a dollar a car load, she could have anything she wanted. She went to the dump every Friday as that was the day before burning and the pickings were the best.

Once my family went to visit her and we all went to the dump to help her get merchandise for the store.

My mother, daddy, sisters, my aunt and I all gleaned treasures from each and every humongous pile of discards from the entire City of San Antonio.

When we got ready to leave the dump, my aunt realized she had lost her keys! All of us retraced our steps in the labyrinth of refuse until my aunt found her keys. Talk about finding a needle in a haystack, she found one in a haystack community. Not only did she find her keys, but she did it in the dark with only a pin light to illuminate her path.

Lefties Have Rights Too

*L*ife is full of embarrassing situations, and mine has not escaped that bit of normalcy. I am a bona fide card-carrying lefty. I am not ashamed of being left-handed, but I am often inconvenienced by it. Face it, this is a right-handed world.

When I was in elementary school, I was always the last one chosen to be on anyone's team. Why? Because I could hit the ball to Kalamazoo, but instead of running to first base, I would most assuredly, always run to third base. Because lefties always gravitate to the left and third base was to the left of the batter's base, causing me to run slap dap into the third baseman.

I learned early in life what it felt like to be body-slammed. I have been on a crash course with kids of every size from the third to the fifth grades.

My daddy, who is a lefty also, would not let me handle a knife at the dinner table until I was fourteen years old. It just looked plain awkward to him.

Camye's Chicken Bye, Bye

My Friend, Camye had just gotten a new house. It was huge and had every conceivable convenience.

She had a state-of-the-art kitchen range, installed in her new home. It was a modular stove with interchangeable components. It was electric. It had a part that allowed for cooking meat on a rotisserie.

Anxious to try it out, Camye put a whole chicken on it and started it up. She sat down to observe the action. She did not realize how long it would take to cook a five pound chicken.

She failed to tuck the bird's wings and it was too late to do it after it started cooking.

When it came time to serve the roasted-to-perfection poultry, she could not bring herself to eat it.

Her reason, She could not eat anything that had been waving bye, bye to her for three hours!

The Virginia Unreel

*O*ur fifth grade class was studying pioneer days, and we decided to put on a play about it.

We made a cardboard covered wagon out of a box that a refrigerator had come in. Then we went to work collecting old implements and costumes for our play.

We rehearsed the Virginia Reel, which is the type of dance pioneers enjoyed, (or so we were told).

There was a boy in my class no one wanted for a partner because he had braces on his legs. He developed polio when he was a baby and could not stand or walk without the clunky shafts of iron supporting his body.

I couldn't dance, so I volunteered to be Bobby's partner. I thought that his clumsiness would make my clumsiness less noticeable, Instead, I discovered Bobby had a very sweet personality. He was polite and patient. He let me lead.

The night of the play, he and I got a standing ovation. It was mostly for him, but I was glad to be his partner. We remained friends for several years.

Jeannie's Invention

*W*hen we were between the ages of six and ten, we lived next door to a vacant lot. The lot was overgrown with Johnson grass that towered over our heads by at least a foot.

We would play hide and seek for hours, just running and squatting in the midst of the weeds.

Jeannie got an idea how she could find the hiders faster. She got her yo-yo and began to swing it around her head, lopping off the tops of the grass.

It was a wonder she didn't kill one of us with that chunk of wood hurling at such high speed.

Years later, we were reminded that if she had realized what she had done, we would have been rich.

The yo-yo string cutting the Johnson grass was predecessor to the weed eater everyone uses today.

Uncle Kelsey Holds The Baby

*U*ncle Kelsey was totally blind. He lost his sight only months before my youngest sister was born. We all felt badly because he would never see her. He loved us kids so much and we surely loved him as well.

Uncle Kelsey was a marvel. He played dominoes even though he could not see his hand. He felt the dots on every tile and the other players would tell him what they had played. Most of the time he would win.

When the new baby was three months old, my next youngest sister got a big rubber doll for Christmas.

We came upon the idea of playing a trick on our good-natured uncle.

Actually, my parents, my uncle's wife, our Aunt Mae, and all us kids were in on this conspiracy to replace the infant with the doll as a practical joke.

They had Uncle Kelsey sit in a comfortable chair and Momma handed him "The Baby."

The joke backfired when he commented, "I bet you don't get much trouble out of this one."

Momma Paints The Kitchen

*T*he war in Korea was ending and things were rough over most of the country.

The price of food was soaring and we had to cut corners any way we could.

Momma made a big pot of pinto beans every week. We ate from that batch until it was gone, then she'd make another.

One time, bean cooking day fell on payday and Momma was out of beans. She went to the store when Daddy got home, which threw her off schedule by several hours.

To speed things up, Momma put the beans in her pressure cooker. This turned out to be a bad move!

The pressure built the steam as usual, but this time it exploded, painting the kitchen with the brown stain of the pinto beans on the walls and ceiling in the area of the stove.

The explosion made a loud noise and sent us kids scrambling under the bed.

With all the talk of war and bombs, we were sure we were in grave danger.

It took us three days to clear the mess from the walls and ceiling, preparing them for repainting.

The kitchen had to be repainted to get the brown stains off the ceiling and walls.

Lock Buttons

*I*f I have a fear of anything, it is the fear of being lost in a crowd. It has happened to me too often in my life and it sends me into sheer panic every time.

I cannot function under those circumstances. I scream, I cry, I stutter, and I freeze up whenever I am separated from the people I am with and I am somewhere other than where I am supposed to be.

Our elementary school was having its usual fall carnival on the asphalt playground at the school. There was a cakewalk and several other games for children to enjoy.

I went on the cakewalk and won a big two-layer frosted pink cake.

I looked around expecting Momma to be there to carry my cake to the car, but she was gone. She had taken Lois to the Potty. I panicked, I hollered, "I'm lost!" In my loud bellowing voice.

When asked to describe my mother all I could think of was that she was wearing her blouse with the novelty buttons shaped like little padlocks.

The principle went from lady to lady looking for someone wearing lock buttons.

He came back rubbing his face, which had been slapped, with the bullhorn in his hand from the cakewalk pleading, "Will the lady with the lock buttons, please come and collect your daughter at the cakewalk booth."

As it turned out, Momma was almost as upset as I was. We took my cake home and enjoyed it that night but not before the lecture on "What to do if you become lost."

No Lemon!

My Sister, Myra was only four years old when my husband and I decided to move back to Louisiana so he could work in the oilfield.

My parents gave us a going away dinner party at a very fine restaurant in downtown Fort Worth. We all ordered steaks and all the trimmings. We all got a huge glass of iced tea. On the edge of each glass was a slice of lemon.

I took mine off and laid it on my bread plate. Myra, who was sitting next to me, picked it up and squeezed it over her sister's tea glass. The juice was dripping down her arm and landed like droplets from her elbow into the glass. I shrieked, "Myra, I didn't want lemon in my tea!" In her sweetest voice, she whispered, "Well, you got it anyway."

My shriek was the only voice the other patrons in that restaurant heard. I was mortified! To this day, I do not take lemon in my tea.

Daddy's Bucket Seat

*A*s mentioned, in earlier chapters, we often had a clunker in our driveway in the process of being overhauled.

Daddy had a car that was almost ready to roll. The only thing holding it up was the seats. He had sent them to be re-upholstered.

Daddy got up to go to work and discovered that the other car would not start. He went to the shed and found the old ice cream freezer and turning it upside down, placed it in the car where the driver's seat should have been. He was not even late to work that day. It wasn't until years later that the so called bucket seat became popular in some sports cars.

The Ottoman Coaster

*B*abysitters are hard to come by, especially if there is no money to spare. This was the case when my two oldest sisters were growing up. My parents would sometimes leave us at home to look after one another while they went grocery shopping.

Once, while they were gone, we discovered that the floor in the living room and dining room was a gradual slope toward the front door. The old house had settled to the point that all of the floors were affected.

We had an ottoman on casters that we used as our rollercoaster car. We took turns riding or pushing that ottoman down the incline, which was the full distance of the two rooms.

When it was my turn, I stuck my feet out in front of me and both my sisters pushed. Our fun came to a crashing halt when my feet knocked a large hole in the wall by the front door.

We quickly got our chores done and rearranged all the living room furniture placing the piano on the other side of the room to cover the hole.

The damage was not discovered until we were preparing to move and Daddy sold the piano to avoid moving it to the new house. By then, my older sister was married, so I got the lecture and the lashing for the both of us.

Flooring Murgatroid

*D*addy had this thing about naming our jalopies. One-step, side pick-up truck, he christened, "Murgatroid."

Since it was a truck, there was not enough room for all of us to ride in the cab. The three of us always rode in the load bed.

We had to hang on tightly, as the old truck delivered a very rough ride, most of the time. Daddy had our safety in mind so he put wooden rails on the truck-bed.

We could then stand up to ride and enjoy the wind whipping through our hair.

We knew where all the big potholes were and made a game of jumping the potholes.

We would hang onto the rails and jump as we approached the bump that was sure to jolt us out of our shoes, if we didn't.

One such jump resulted in my foot going through the floor of the truck where the wooden floor had been damaged by heavier previous cargo. I was not hurt but I was sufficiently imprinted with the message that I was to sit or stand, but not jump while riding in the back of a truck!

It Runs In The Family

My mother's brother, Albert had two sons at the time. One of them, Gary was about four years old. He Had never heard that he had an uncle Delbert, Neither had he ever met him.

The child really knew nothing of the man. One day out of the blue, Uncle Delbert cam to call on Uncle Albert and his family.

Delbert was dressed in his finest attire. He wore a three piece wool suit and very shiny shoes. On his head he wore a nice gray felt hat with a wide hatband of the deepest purple. He was, as they say, quite dapper.

Gary took one look at Uncle Delbert and said, "Take off your hat so I can see your bald head."

The gentleman reached up dutifully and removed his hat. Under the hat was the shiniest bald head Gary had ever seen. The boy laughed. He was not making fun of the naked scalp, but was laughing because Uncle Delbert was bald, just like Gary's dad.

Like My Hat?

The year was 1948. The second round of post-world war II was well defined. The first baby boomers were toddlers of toilet training age.

Some genius decided that these toddlers in their terrible two's needed their own scaled down potty to be trained on. He must have used a G.I. coffee mug for a model because the new teaching tool resembled a larger version of one.

Momma put my sister, Jeannie on the new potty and went to answer the door. When she returned, Jeannie had put the potty on her head and was gleefully parading around the bathroom like a strutting bandleader.

Momma tried to remove the potty from my sister's head but it was stuck. Momma tried baby oil, mayonnaise, butter, and cold cream but nothing loosened that potty from my Sissie's noggin.

Momma was so embarrassed, she wrapped the child in the long coat and took her to the doctor. When she opened the door of the office, there sat four other mothers with toddlers in their laps. Each baby had a potty on its head!

My Un-Boyfriend

*D*ennis Kemp was in my sister's seventh grade class. About the middle of the school year, Dennis became very ill. I do not remember what his affliction was. But I do know he was bed-ridden for a long time.

Jeannie started calling him every day to give him the class assignments. Sometimes, he would do them, sometimes he was too sick to do anything.

Finally, he just quit altogether. Although he stopped doing the lessons, he continued to call my sister. As soon as she walked in the door from school every day, the phone would ring. Somehow he knew the exact time she got home from school.

They would talk for a few minutes before she would make up an excuse to hang up.

When Jeannie lost all interest in talking to Dennis, I took over and answered the phone each day when we got home from school.

I had nothing better to do, so I listened to Dennis talk about everything 13 year old boys like to talk about.

Dennis asked me to be his girlfriend and I said, "Yes." This was my very first boyfriend ever.

I never saw him and he never saw me. This was strictly a telephone romance. Somewhat like a forerunner of today's cyber sweethearts.

We talked on the phone daily for about two months. Then all of a sudden, he quit calling.

Several months later Dennis' dad died. My sister and I went to his funeral, as friends of Dennis'. I saw him for the first time then.

I think every girl in the seventh grade was at that funeral.

Dennis was still ill but he was gorgeous! He was the handsomest boy I had ever seen. I thought if he'd seen me, he probably would not have asked me to be his girlfriend. I knew I was not special to him. Evidenced by the gaggle of girls that surrounded him at his father's funeral.

On the phone, he made me feel special and for that, I thank him. I know Dennis is long gone. But I will always remember him fondly.

Bait and Switch

*L*iving on the Bayou has its advantage. I could go fishing anytime I pleased. Often I would fish from my kitchen window.

I would go out and put out my line and go back into the house to do my housework.

One time, I was making outfits for my mother, myself, and my older sister.

I had been sewing for the biggest part of the day. I was hand stitching the hem on one of the skirts when I noticed the bobber on my line was not visible. I ran out to "reel him in." Just as I cleared the water with the fish it spat the hook and was gone. He and the worm I had for bait were somewhere between Raceland and Lockport.

I have a habit of stiffening new thread by placing the end in my mouth then threading my needle. Worms on fish hooks are not the same…believe me!

My Weirdest Dream

*W*hen I was fourteen, I had a crush on one of the most unattractive boys in my eight grade class. He was a tall, red-headed, freckle-faced, clumsy boy. His name was Bobby Miller. I was in love. He was nice to me so I thought he was in love with me too.

One night, I had a dream about him. I dreamed, I had long green hair. I was with Bobby and we were walking down the street holding hands. A car came out of nowhere and hit Bobby. He lay in the street, bloody and unconscious.

I tried to get the license plate number of the car that hit him. But each time I tried to memorize it, the numbers changed until the car was out of sight.

Bobby had landed on the end of my hair. Which pinned me down so I couldn't go for help, and the street was deserted. When I tried to get up my hair stretched. I went into a building and found a pair of scissors on a window sill. I used them to cut my hair.

I opened a door to see if there was anyone there who might be able to help me with Bobby and get him to a hospital.

The room was dark with the exception of a few candles. It was also empty, except for a large box in the middle of the floor.

I walked over to the box, opened the top and looked in. Bobby was inside the coffin, dead.

I woke up screaming! After that, I never dreamed about Bobby again. Soon, I had a crush on another boy.

After 8 years, that dream is still as vivid now as it was that night.

If Ben Is Bo: Who Is Luke?

*B*en was a five year old student in my kindergarten class at the school I'd taught for one year.

He had a very active imagination. The first thing he did was give me a false name when I was making my attendance chart. He told me his name was Billy Bunch.

The TV show, "The Dukes of Hazzard" was in its hay day during that time. For days at a time, Ben would only answer, if I called him Bo. No amount of reminding him of his actual name got any results.

Finally, I told him to leave Bo at home or don't come to school. The next day, not being bothered by reality Ben, came to school anyway.

For that entire day he was not Bo, he wasn't even Luke, Jesse, or Daisey. He was, General Lee. The only word he said the whole day was, "Varoom!"

Windwalkers

*T*exas winters presented a problem because we didn't have adequate heat in the ram-shackled house where we lived. We only had two space heaters. One in Daddy and Momma's room and one in our room. The heat from the stove kept the kitchen warm and the bathroom had no heating elements at all. We relished taking a very hot bath to keep warm in the bathroom.

One winter, the clothes dryer broke down. Momma had us hang the clothes on the line outside in the backyard.

We always had to hang Daddy's pants by the cuffs and let gravity put the crease in them.

A hard freeze came one evening just after I had hung a large wash load on the line. The following morning, all the laundry was frozen stiff. A brisk wind came up, Momma looked out the kitchen window just in time to see Daddy's pants walking across the yard.

Good Save

*A*s teenagers, Jeannie and I often invited our boyfriends over for dinner and we would cook for them. We usually had hot dogs or hamburgers.

I was trying hard to shed my tomboy persona. I wanted to prove I could be a good homemaker and behave in a feminine manner.

I was making my boyfriend a hamburger I thought he wanted. I sat down beside him and shoved the plate in his direction. I had not yet eaten. He came first, or so I thought.

He shoved it back at me so hard that the burger took flight from the plate and landed in my lap.

I was wearing pants at the time. I slammed my knees together and caught the sandwich between them. My quick reflexes saved the hamburger, but it shattered all hopes of shedding my tomboy image.

Un-dishing The Dirt

My sister, Lois has always had a thing for plants. It was no surprise that her mother-in-law gave her a houseplant for a housewarming gift when she and her husband bought their new house.

The kitchen window as the perfect atrium, as it featured a bay window with a pie shelf.

Lois placed several plants in the space the window provided. One such plant was a small but healthy geranium.

One morning Lois got up to make coffee. She found a small pile of dirt on the kitchen counter. Not knowing where it came from, she scooped it up with a spoon and put it in the geranium pot.

The next morning, the dirt appeared on the counter again. Lois scooped up the dirt and put it in the same pot as before. But each morning she continued to be met with the same scenario.

One day, we actually made visual contact with a small mole that had been transported in the potting soil that had come in with the potted geranium. The rodent came out at night to look for food. He was living under the plant and un-dishing the dirt every evening.

Ducks On Parade

*O*ur family lived in an old ram shackled house on the south side of Fort Worth for seven of my growing up years.

We had a large lot, that was covered with about eight acres of mostly Johnson grass.

The front yard, the house, and the back yard where we played was on the front four acres.

The four acres behind that was for our menagerie of livestock of goats, chickens, pigeons, and rabbits, consecutively.

At one time, we had eight ducks occupying the coop and its enclosure. It was my job to feed the ducks each morning before I went to school.

I did my chore, not realizing the ducks were gone. That afternoon I was confronted by my father. He was angry and certain I had left the gate unlocked. I was punished and denied dessert that night.

The next morning, we were awakened by the noise of seemingly happy white ducks waddling up our long driveway back to their pen.

We never did learn where they had been. After that incident, I was always careful to double check the gate lock.

Jack Benny Escaped

I had a large fish tank and a variety of tropical fish and sea life. One of which was a fiddler crab I called Jack Benny.

My sister Lois and I shared an apartment while my husband was on a job in Louisiana.

He was to send for me when he found a place for us to live.

Lois' daughter, Lori was almost two. One day I looked into the fish tank and noticed Jack Benny was gone! A thorough search failed to locate the creature.

We looked everywhere we though a crab might be. We looked in the tub, we looked under the sink, and even in the trash can. Jack Benny was nowhere to be found.

Lois offered Lori her bottle but the child refused to take it. Upon closer examination Lois realized Lori had something in her mouth. Lois gently squeezed the girl's cheeks until she opened her mouth. Lori slowly rolled out her tongue. Perched on it, was Jack Benny.

He survived the adventure and was put back into the tank to be reunited with his friends.

Daddy's Bicycle Factory

*O*ne Christmas, my sisters and I got 'new' bikes. For weeks before that time, Daddy would go to the garage after work and there he would stay until supper time.

We were curious to know what he was doing, but we dared not go into the garage. We knew he was doing something but were not sure we wanted to be a part of it. It sounded like too much work.

Shortly after the visits to the garage stopped and all the noise of tools in operation ceased, Daddy presented each of us with a new bike.

The only new part was the tires. The rest were assorted parts from an assortment of about ten different broken bikes.

When he was finished, to brighten them up, he painted each one. He did not have enough of any one color of paint, so he improvised.

My bike was John Deere green and yellow. Jeannie's was blue and red. Lois' bike was orange and white.

They were all one of a kind bikes that no self-respecting thief would ever try to take. We could ride anywhere and not feel the need for a bike chain. The bike factory closed permanently in 1955.

I Got A Fence Bite

On any given Wednesday evening around seven, there was an aggregation of young people in the parking lot of our church, running around and playing games while the older folk were having a teacher's meeting.

There were five Lunsford's, six Neal's, six Richardson's, three Corey's, six Kelly's and three Herriott's.

There were also a few single kids with no siblings. Mostly, we played family against family.

My present husband, Donald was one such single. He was almost always the 'Monster,' whenever we played chase. The family with the most members that had not gotten caught by the time we were called in for church, was the winner.

Once, Donald was chasing us, (me in particular) as he knew I was exceedingly slow. I ran behind the outhouse, (yes we had an outhouse at our church).

I became entangled in some barbed wire and snagged the back of my left knee. It required eight stitches. I think of this as the first thing my husband ever gave me!

The Flying Dutchman Catastrophe

𝒯he third grade was the worst for me. I was tall, skinny and probably the most un athletic child in my class. I could not catch a ball, jump a rope, or run.

One game we played was called Flying Dutchman. All the children formed a circle holding hands. One pair of kids walked around the outside of the circle and chopped the hands apart of the ones they wanted to challenge.

The chosen ones clasped hands again to chase the first pair around the circle. The four kids ran until the first pair got back to the opening or the second pair tagged them.

The time I got paired with Shirley Millirons, is a day I shall never forget.

My feet touched the ground maybe four times in that entire circle navigation. If she did not go on to the Olympics, I would be greatly surprised. I do not like anyone but me to control speed at which my body is hurled through space.

The Woody Wagon Taxi

My uncle Tom had a woody. It has since become a classic automobile but in the early years, it was not regarded as a desirable make of car. Only a few had one and they were less than proud of it.

My sister Jeannie, our cousin Ann and I played taxi in it every time we went to see Uncle Tom and Aunt Dorothy.

One of us got to be the driver and the other two were the passengers. We did a lot of role playing as the paying passengers of the old wagon.

I am not even sure due to our status of preschoolers at the time, how we even knew what a taxi was.

Uncle Tom had that wagon for years and when he decided to sell it, it was as if he was selling an old friend.

Uncle Tom died in 1957. I miss him and his "Woody" whenever I think of him.

Twenty Dollars and Sixty Cents

I was sixteen years old when my parents had a produce stand in south Fort Worth.

This was a family business and we all worked really hard. I was not good with basic arithmetic and so often the till would come up short. Customers waited until I was on duty to come in.

I would keep the change and give them back the price of the purchase. I knew I had to account for every dime, so when one rolled under the potato bin, I went after it.

Not only did I find the dime I lost, but I also found two quarters and a faded twenty dollar bill. There is no way of knowing how long it had been there.

Momma and Daddy used the twenty to go to San Antonio to see my Uncle Jack for the last time. He died soon after. For a long time, I felt robbed of the money I'd found. But today, I feel as if I'd given my parents a gift, as Uncle Jack was very special.

The Angel's Accident

$\mathcal{K}$aren was in the kindergarten class I taught back in 1983. She was four years old. Her mother also worked in the school with the older students in another part of the building.

Every once in a while Karen, being the youngest child in the class, cried for her mother. I would take her to her mother and shortly thereafter, Karen would be brought back to class ready to be the excellent student she was.

It was near Christmas time and we were planning to present a Christmas play for the parents and church members. Danny would play the part of Joseph. Dawn, was Mary, Tonya was a shepherd, Ben was a wiseman and Karen was an angel.

Casting was no easy task because of the limited number of students I had.

We were in the sanctuary rehearsing the play. I was to be the narrator and the children were to be still and quiet.

We made it almost to the end before Ben spoke up. "Ms. Brown, the angel pooped her pants" I learned that day, you don't instruct a newly toilet trained child to be still and quiet for more than ten minutes.

My Appetite

*A*s a young child, I developed a mild anemia because I was such a picky eater. I did not like anything green or any kind of meat. I did like fried chicken, though.

I also ate cereal, pancakes, mashed potatoes and every kind of dessert we had. None of the items on my personal menu were iron efficient enough to combat my anemia.

I was taken to the doctor because I was not as active as I had been and Momma just knew there was something dreadfully wrong with me.

The doctor prescribed a Geritol type liquid called Stewart's formula for me that was supposed to increase my appetite. That stuff tasted horrible. It had the flavor of burnt sugar.

After about six doses of the awful elixir, I finally told Momma, "I don't need any more of that stuff, I get hungry just smelling it."

Firewalker

*T*he meanest thing my husband's brother ever did to him occurred when he was about seven years old.

The boys were at the back of the house burning a pile of rubble that had been collected in the cleanup process before their dad could build a new room onto their house.

The older boy challenged the younger boy to run through the fire. He teased the child, calling him 'chicken' and other uncomplimentary names. The older boy offered to demonstrate to his little brother how to jump the flames.

He did just that, he jumped. However it appeared to the smaller boy, his brother had indeed walked through the tongues of fire, unscathed.

The youthful sibling, not to be outdone, walked into the fire as he had seen his older brother do. The heat reached his feet and he froze in his tracks. When he came out, he ran to the house and before he could go inside he stopped at the dog's water dish and plunged his feet into the cold liquid.

Later as the doctor was bandaging the boy's badly burned feet, he said the dog's water may very well have saved Don's feet.

As punishment for duping his younger brother to do something that dangerous and stupid, my future brother-in-law and my future husband, became inseparable. It was not by choice but by parental decree. At least until Don was able to walk again.

Elbow Biter

*W*hen my husband, Donald was fourteen years old, my sister Lois was seven. Donald was Jeannie's Boyfriend at the time. Lois had this thing about always wanting to be the center of attention. She inserted herself into every situation. Donald thought she was a pest. He thought I was a pest, too. Lois and I were in his way of romancing Jeannie.

Lois liked to tickle Don and make him laugh. He had a pleasant robust laugh and he did it often.

One day, Don refused to laugh to see if Lois would then leave him alone. She sank her teeth into his elbow and hung on like a dog with rabies.

She thought if she couldn't make him laugh, she'd make him cry. He thought if he laughed she'd feel victorious and let go. He did not get the results he was after and neither did she. Today the two are very good friends. Donald has been her brother-in-law for more than thirty-three years.

Aunt Jo And The Spider Web

We all knew Aunt Jo was just a tad crazy. She reacted in a most unusual way to almost everything. The things one might think would upset her, she took in stride. The most subtle events she went mental over.

Once Grandma sent her to the garage to get a box of canning jars so she could put up a few quarts of preserves. She did not see the humongous web over the door initially. However, as she turned to leave the garage, she ran smack dab into it. There was no spider to be reckoned with, so she should have just kept going. But not my beloved Aunt Jo! She shrieked and tossed the jars as if they were a volleyball. She twisted and turned and jumped like a marionette on a hundred strings. Some of her body action seemed to be impossible. She fought her way out of the web which none of us were able to see from the house. It appeared she was having some kind of tantrum. The spider web dance was indeed a strange sight to see, even if it was Aunt Jo who did it.

Sparkle's Lunch

My husband's ex-stepmother had given us a beautiful full blooded Yorkshire Terrier. We named him Sparkle because he was so happy and bouncy. He was bursting with joy.

It seemed, he wanted to please everyone. He weighed only a couple of pounds fully grown.

We had to have him shaved so we could rescue him from a tick infestation that could have killed him. He looked weird. Everyone who saw him wanted to know what he was.

Daddy always had a habit of keeping his pants on the floor beside his bed so if he had to get up during the night, he would be covered. (He was a very modest man).

Daddy got up one Sunday morning and made his usual pancakes. After everyone had eaten, Daddy gave Sparkle a pancake with syrup on it. The little dog was grateful and ate his fill. He had a large bite left and carried it into the master bedroom, no one even noticed it.

Daddy went into the bedroom to get dressed for church. He put his dress pants on, only to discover the zipper was stuck. Rather than deal with that, he reached down and got his old standby pair of pants and put them on.

He felt something in his pocket but assumed it was his handkerchief and forgot about it.

At church he needed to sneeze, so he reached into his pants pocket to get his 'shooter,' as he called it. Daddy pulled out a handful of Sparkle's lunch dripping with syrup.

Timex...The Watch Dog

My husband and I had a German Shepherd dog we called Timex. This was a dog who'd earned his name. He would wait for Don to go to work and then he would jump the fence.

Try as I might, I could not get that dog to go back into the yard. He had free reign of the homestead until he heard Don's car coming up the road. Timex would jump back over the fence moments before Don turned onto the driveway.

It took a long time for me to convince Don that Timex ever left that enclosure.

One day, he cut the engine of the car and coasted to the driveway in an effort to catch Timex jumping the fence. The dog saw the car at the end of the driveway and like a Gazelle, he hurdled the fence as if it wasn't even there.

She was standing at the gate waiting for Don to rub her head before she came into the house. "Well honey," Don said, "Timex is a watch dog. He waits for me to come home before he jumps back into the yard. On second thought, He's not a watchdog, he is a wait dog."

The Demise of the Chirpy

*A*nimals don't fair very well around our family. When I was five, I was playing hide and seek with my sisters and some friends of ours in their backyard.

There were farm fowl everywhere. There was an old momma hen with a large brood of chicks, a guinea or two and a peacock all running loose in the yard.

To avoid being found and tagged, I ran as fast as I could to the safety zone. While running, I tripped and fell flat on my face, causing all the baby chicks to scatter.

There was one that did not survive. The impact of my chubby little body falling on him will forever be remembered with a wave of sadness each time I think of that poor tragic little chicken.

No Blue Jeans

I was my practice to lay out my husband's work clothes every morning while he was in the shower.

I always hung his jeans over the kitchen door to dry before going to bed. One night I'd forgotten to wash them until very late.

The next morning, they were still damp, so I gave him a pair I had washed the day before. They were his last pair of khaki pants.

He went to work wearing the worn-out britches. As I was doing my housework, I was listening to the local radio station as usual. An announcement came over the radio of a fatal truck/train wreck at Oak Grove Plantation Road.

That was the exact location my husband was scheduled to work that day. No names were given until next of kin could be notified.

The bits and pieces of information given over the radio throughout the day scared me to death that I would be the widow Brown.

It was announced, the body would be taken to Raceland Funeral Home, which was directly across the stretch from our home.

I waited as long as I could before hurriedly going across the street to that funeral home to find out if my husband was the truck driver that had been killed.

I rang the bell, the door was opened by an older gentleman. I told him of my concerns. They said they were sorry, but they were not at liberty to give out any information.

I asked if they could just describe the man for me to ease my mind. He was about thirty…………………………....check
He was a large man…………….check
He had brown hair……………....check
With each piece of information came an uneasy dread. He was wearing cowboy boots…………………………check
He wore a blue shirt…………….gulp!!
…and blue jeans!!!!!!!

Kylie's First Fishing Trip

My parents lived in a mobile home community in East Texas. They had access to a large lake that had several varieties of fish.

The sand bass were biting so some of us went to the pier to try our luck.

The men were going to do the fishing and the women were going to keep the kids entertained and away from the water. There was no boat. The men had to fish from the bank of the pier. The playground was far enough away to be safe, but close enough so that we could seem to be a part of the experience. We could see when one of the men caught a fish.

My niece Kymie, was in my arms as I walked to the pier to ask the fishermen if they were ready for a bologna sandwich yet.

My brother-in-law lifted his rod high in the air and there was a three inch minnow hooked on the line. My niece squealed with glee, "He got one, he got one!"

The Naked Catfish

My husband and I lived on the bank of Bayou Lafourche. We had a pier jutting out into the Bayou about twenty feet. We would go fishing anytime the mood would strike us.

Often I would go put out a line and go back inside to do dishes and watch for a bite from the kitchen window.

Once my husband caught a large catfish. He nailed it to a board to skin it and clean it. He always skinned them first, then cut the heads off. He had skinned one side and was flipping him over to do the other side when the fish fell back into the Bayou.

Surprisingly, the fish swam away. Can you imagine the look on the face of the next fisherman who caught that catfish?

My First Kiss

*W*hen I was twelve years old and in the seventh grade my sister was invited to her first boy/girl birthday party. Of course I was required to go with her to be Momma's little snitch. We went to the party, and the games began! We played Spin the Bottle, Truth or Dare, and a game called Seven Minutes in Heaven.

In this game, a boy and girl went into a closet together, and the door was shut. After the children outside of the door counted the minutes, the door was jerked open. The idea was to catch them doing something.

Another game was called slap, kiss or hug. In this one the boys and girls were paired up at random. When it came my turn I was paired with the cutest boy there. I wanted him to kiss me. I wanted to kiss him. But…I remember what Momma always said. "If a boy gets fresh with you, slap him and run." So he kissed me…and I slapped him! Thanks to Momma, I may have ruined what might have been a more pleasant memory.

Borrowed Britches

*O*ur favorite week-end pastime was to spend Sunday afternoon between church services with our friends. Sometimes they would come to our house, other times we would go to theirs.

Often we would walk the six miles to the Sunday matinee at the Plaza or Poly Theater.

When my sister and her boyfriend were fourteen, Momma made sure I was always with them because she knew I would tell if they did anything they shouldn't do. I was a major tattle-tale.

One Sunday afternoon the three of us went to the park to play. My sister's boyfriend had borrowed a pair of dress pants of his dad's to wear to church. He did not bring a change of clothes as he usually did. His dad cautioned him to be careful with those pants.

The boy bent over in the creek to get a closer look at a crayfish. He heard a dreadful sound as the seam of his borrowed trousers split from waist band to inseam. His body was exposed. He tied the sleeves of his jacket around his waist and we headed back to our house. He was lucky on two counts. One, he had a jacket and two, the pants could be repaired.

Earshinditioners And Ambades

I am sure most family members have or had a child who seemed to have a language all her/his own.

The creative one in our family was Lois. She gave everything an identifying title. Earshinditioner was Air Conditioner, Ambage was Band-aid, fitter retter was refrigerator and so on.

Her most unique title was when she dubbed the piano, pee-nanner.

It may have outdone her one time, and that was before she was born. Momma was saying words and I was repeating them as best I could. She was saying words like, Grandma, Daddy, Love, Cookie, Water, and other beginner words.

Then she started in on animals. I was doing fine until she threw Hippopotamus at me. I echoed, "Bon Bon Bottomus."

No One Will Ever Know

This may qualify as one of the lies My Momma told me.

I was twelve years old. I had just had minor surgery on my big toes to correct my ingrown toenails. The nails had been extracted and the bare toes were extra sensitive, so I wore saddle shoes to school and to church.

This was alright with me as I was quite the tomboy. I had not yet discovered my feminine side.

It was close to Valentine's Day, and the twelve to fifteen year old's at church were going to have a "Sweetheart Banquet." I had no such sweetheart, so Momma asked a friend of hers to allow her son to be my "date."

I borrowed a gown from a friend at school. I had my hair done at the beauty shop. For the first time, I was permitted to get a perm.

I couldn't get my feet in dress shoes, due to the bandages on my toes. Momma said, "Wear your saddle shoes, honey. No one will ever know."

I put the shoes on and stood in front of the hall mirror. My dress was long enough to prevent the shoes from being seen. I was thrilled.

At the banquet, there was a presentation of couples. Each couple walked to the center of the stage, bowed and curtsied as their names were announced. Afterward, the couples took their seats at the banquet table.

When it was my turn, as I was ascending the steps to the stage, I tripped on the hem of my gown. I tried desperately to regain my balance by taking a few more steps. But I was unable to and fell flat on my face at center stage. All eyes were on me. The tail of my dress flew up and landed at my knees, showing the very shoes I had attempted to hide.

My feet were in the air and my saddle shoes were exposed for all the world to see.

I did not see the boy I was partnered with for one whole year.

Once again, he was asked to escort me to the annual banquet. His country boy reply was, "Yes, but only if I can wear my cowboy boots." As it turned out, he was not embarrassed by my shoes or the fall I took. He just wanted to wear comfortable shoes too.

Rita Fay's Treasure Hunt

*T*here were about ten of us kids playing games in the back of the Lunsford's house. One of the games we played involved all of us holding hands in a long line and running. The leader would snake through the yard as fast as he could. The object was to lose his tail, (which was the last person in the line).

The rule was, if anyone broke the chain, everyone from the point where the chain was broken, to the end of the line would be out of the game.

The leader was running swiftly. He was slinging kids everywhere. The little kids were always last because they could not hang on or run as fast as necessary to keep from becoming separated.

Rita Fay was at the tail end of the line. She was being whipped and slung in every direction. Finally she could no longer hang on and released her feeble grip from me. She landed head-first into an empty trash can. Only her legs from the knees to her feet were visible. Her mother yelled from the kitchen door, "Rita Fay, get out of there!" The girl replied, "In a minute, I can't find my gum!

The Apple Crate Bathtub

*O*ur family went without many of the modern conveniences when I was growing up. One such convenience was a bathtub. We had no indoor plumbing and not much opportunity to take a sit, soak and soap bath.

Nevertheless, Momma saw to it that we were clean. We used a number 2 washtub to wash off the West Texas dust.

Momma was unable to fit in the tub as she was pregnant with my sister, Lois.

From April to August, we all went to the creek once a week, (more often if it was extremely hot) to take a bath in the cool clear water.

Daddy fashioned an innertube and an apple crate in such a way, that three inches of water flowed into the crate. He tied a rope to the innertube and the other end to a tree. Then, he put my sister and I in the crate so he and Momma could enjoy their baths.

We moved to a house with indoor facilities shortly after Lois was born. I had a hard time adjusting to warm water baths.

What Was Said Is Not What He Thought Was Said

*A*dults have no way of knowing what their children hear, or predicting how a child will perceive what he or she hears the adult say.

My sister, Lois was looking for a lawyer to handle her divorce. She complained to my mother that she couldn't find one she could afford.

Lois made a comment that if she were rich, there would be lawyers coming out of the woodwork.

Lois' son had come in from playing outdoors with his friends. He only came in to the kitchen where his mother and grandmother were talking and sipping coffee. He said nothing.

The boy went back outside to play. One of his friends said, "let's go play in the woods." My nephew replied, "Not me! There are monsters and lawyers in there." Four year old's, take everything so literally.

Footprints On The Well

We lived in a two room tarpaper shack in what was then a very rural area of Fort Worth.

We had a dilapidated old outhouse, a number two washtub and a 30 foot well that comprised our plumbing facilities.

We only had running water the time the bees chased Daddy back to the house one summer.

Daddy had collected a hundred or more nice colorful flat stones and petrified wood pieces to make a cylinder above the hole which was our well.

Daddy worked the better part of one whole day carefully placing each stone where it would best fit to create a four foot high well shaft.

He reinforced the cylinder with shards of wood and applied a thin coat of sacked cement to the inside with a mop. The well was really pretty.

Daddy was about to throw out the remainder of the cement when he decided to use it to make an apron instead, so if the ground was wet, it would not become slippery around the new well.

We had been watching Daddy from the kitchen door and were excited when he called to us to come see the well. He lifted us on his shoulders and carried us to the well. He set us down in the wet cement of the apron and we left our footprints there.

I remember when I was 17 years old, Daddy went back to that old house and got those foot prints. He placed them in the flower bed of the new house. He has moved twice since then and he has taken those footprints with him every place he moved.

It is strange what people place sentimental value on in the course of their lives. Daddy is almost eighty and he still has the chuck of cement with his young daughters' footprints. I am so glad he had that happy accident.

Evelyn's New Shoes

*E*velyn was a girl about our age whose family attended our church. The family was not very well off so it was a really special occasion when any of the children got anything new.

One Sunday morning the schooler arrived at church after a long absence due to the children having chicken pox.

All the kids rushed to greet Evelyn and her brother, Patooty. I never knew his real name and how he got his nickname, is not fit for this story.

Anyway, Evelyn stepped out of the car and bent down to wipe her patent leather shoes with her hanky. She announced, "Wait a minute, let me wipe them off first."

It never occurred to Evelyn that we'd missed her. We were there to see her and paid no attention to her shoes.

Where's Gene?

*M*omma wanted to go to the movies with her friends. She could not find a suitable baby sitter for watch me and my sister, so she took us with her. She cautioned us both to be very quiet. I was still on the bottle, so I was soon fast asleep in the dark theater. However, my sister was wide awake.

The movie that was playing was a Gene Autry western. There was a lot of singing in the movie. There were also a lot of blazing guns and more than a few horse chasing scenes.

In one scene, Gene ran behind a huge boulder as a cover to fight off the bad guys. My sister stood up in her seat and shouted as loudly as she could, "I know where he is but I ain't gonna tell you."

The Bench-Legged Fiest

We lived on two acres of land that had two separate paths and two rooms. One path led to the outhouse and the other path led to the well. The two rooms consisted of a kitchen and an adequate bedroom where the four of us slept. Momma and Daddy had a double bed and my sister and I slept in separate cribs.

My parents, my sisters and I all crowded into those two little rooms. It is good that we were small. Jeannie was four, I was three and Lois was a newborn.

We lived on a dirt road that seemed to be a dead end but it wasn't. There were three more houses but they could not be seen from the road.

People would drop off unwanted dogs and puppies near our house. They found their way to our door and refused to leave. Momma threatened them with a broom, to no avail.

One of our acquisitions was called Mickey. He was truly a mixed breed. He was born with his hind legs disjointed at his hips. This pitiful little pup was like a live doll for us. We babied him to pieces.

A friend of our dad's asked him what breed Mickey was. Daddy said, "He was a bench-legged fiest. The man said, "I gotta get me one of those."

My Treasured Pink Birds

*E*veryone has a treasure. Something that has great monetary or sentimental value. I have a pink ceramic planter that depicts two birds on a nest.

The nest area is the plant space behind the birds. I don't know that it has much value to anyone but me, but I will never part with it because my grandmother gave it to me.

When my sisters and I were very young we would visit Grandma every Saturday. Sometimes she would come home with us to spend the night so she could go to church with us on Sunday morning.

Grandma always put her pennies in the bird's nest during the week and when we would come visit, she gave us the pennies to buy candy at the store up the street.

Sometimes, there would be over a dollar's worth of change in those bird's little nest. Once there were so many, that she had to put some of them loose on the shelf where the birds were kept.

The birds are carefully washed every so often. They are kept in a prominent place in every home we call ours. They may be worth only pennies, but to me the memories and the person they represent are priceless. Grandma passed away at the age of ninety-three.

Romeo Gets A Pedicure

*O*ur canary, Romeo had a problem. We ran out of gravel paper for his cage. He had no way of trimming his talons when they grew too long. This made it difficult for him to grip his perch.

I kept forgetting to buy more of the bird's necessary grooming aids, so his talons got quite long and curved. He could no longer walk on the floor of the birdcage. When he sat on his perch, he would slide off as his grip was not tight enough to hold on with the long talons.

I decided to trim his 'nails' with the manicure clippers, but I could not find them anywhere. I took the bird to the kitchen sink and carefully washed his little feet. Then I delicately bit each of his talon tips to a comfortable length and put him back into his cage. He appeared to be grateful that I was willing to do such an unusual act. That was how Romeo got a pedicure.

The Cat And The Cottontails

My folks had an old tom cat named Tiger. Tiger was a sweetheart. He never was any trouble. He would come home with a few bumps and scratches every once in a while, but nothing major.

He liked to go hunting for mice in the field behind our house. Sometimes, he would trek to the park and stalk the woods for birds and other small morsels of rodent type delights.

One morning, he came home with a tiny bit of hairless livestock in his mouth. He brought it to me and dropped it at my feet. He left and I realized that the gift was a baby cottontail rabbit. Several minutes later, he Tiger came back with another one.

There were three baby bunnies delivered directly to me that day. I put them in my fuzzy house slippers to keep them warm and fed them condensed milk from a match stick.

They grew quickly and Tiger tried to be a mama to them. We released them into the woods as soon as they were old enough to survive on their own. Cats are very strange animals.

Can God Do Anything?

*E*very afternoon at two o'clock, Momma would take the baby into the bedroom to nap with her until the school kids got home at four.

The bedroom window on the West wall was bathed in sunlight at that time of day. The window on the North wall of the room was always dark and shadowy.

My sister was lying next to my mother squirming and loudly sighing preventing Momma from getting any rest.

"Honey, be still and go to sleep, "Momma said."

"Momma, can God do anything?" The baby asked.

"Why, yes he can." Momma sleepily replied.

"Then would you ask him to move the sun over to the other window. It's in my eyes!" Requested the clever three year old.

Momma played possum and pretended to be asleep in hopes that the baby would do likewise.

When the older children came home from school, she quietly slipped out of bed and tip toed into the kitchen to make them a snack.

When she returned to check on the baby, she discovered, the sun indeed had shifted away from the window. The baby woke up and began to clap her hands, saying, "Thank you God, Thank you God." Momma knew exactly why she was giving thanks to God.

Our Baby Can Tell Time

*M*omma and her friend Betty Ann had daughters about the same age. Linda was only a few weeks younger than my sister, Jeannie. Betty Ann was always bragging about how smart Linda was and how pretty she was and how advanced for her age she was. Momma was really tired of hearing it.

It would not have been so irritating except Betty Ann always made a remark to put down Jeannie's progress.

The two babies were less than two years old at the time. Jeannie had learned to look at the nearest clock and upon request, she would say "it's 10:40." No matter what time it was, Jeanie would always give the same answer when asked what time it was.

Betty Ann came over one morning for coffee at Momma's cordial invitation. Momma watched the clock ever so slyly until ten-forty. Then she asked Jeannie, "What time is it?" Jeannie toddled over to the clock over the mantle, placed her hands on her hips, cocked her head to the right, then to the left and said, "It's 10:40."

Betty Ann picked Linda up and left in a huff. She came back an hour later with her sister-in-law as a witness, so Momma had to 'fess up." Although Betty Ann continued to brag about her daughter; at least she did cease to make critical comments that implied that her daughter was smarter than my sister.

The Day It Rained Frogs

In the summer of 1955, it rained frogs. Thousands of them fell in about the span of an hour. They hit the ground so hard, their little bellies popped on impact. It was a wonder they survived.

We gathered every vessel we could find to hold them. My sister and I collected five hundred and eighty little frogs. We had shoe boxes, an old coffee pot, a small ice chest and a cigar box all filled to capacity with the tiny creatures from the sky.

This phenomenon does not repeat itself often. I did not learn until years later that frog spores are sometimes carried into the atmosphere with the condensation of water and incubate in the clouds. When the frogs develop and become heavy enough they fall back to the earth as baby frogs.

Calf Licked

*F*arm animals can be scary creatures to a child who has not been around a farm. Baby animals of any kind hold the fascination of kids no matter where they live. Although one may cringe at the idea of petting a heifer, one will rise to the opportunity to hold or pet a newborn calf.

I went to my friend Charles birthday party. We were served cake and ice cream. I made a mess with my ice cream and got the cold sticky stuff all over the front of my dress.

The party ended and when my parents came to get me, we all went down to the barn to see the new calf. The Momma cow was not at all amused by us or even gracious enough to come to the fence. The calf however, seemed particularly interested in me.

He wrapped his long tongue around the cloth which was my dress and would not let go.

I screamed to my Momma, "He's trying to eat me, Momma." The calf was drawn to me by the ice cream on my clothes. I had no choice but to stand there and let him lick the dress clean.

Aunt Jo Finds A Fifty

Aunt Jo was always finding things. Some of the things she found were valuable, some were junk, but valuable to her. A box with a lid was an especially good find. Discarded purses were a favorite acquisition. One never knows what one might find in an old pocketbook.

Aunt Jo found things mainly because she was always looking. Once she found a brand new man's watch still in the plastic case at the dump. Most likely it had accidentally been tossed out with the wrapping papers after a birthday party or something.

She sold the watch to a friend who needed a gift for her dad for Father's day. She used the money to buy more broken toys.

One day, Aunt Jo mentioned she'd like to find a twenty dollar bill. She was asked if she had lost one, she said, "No, but I'd sure like to find one." God must have known about the economy inflation, because Aunt Jo found a fifty dollar bill.

Guillotined!

*B*efore my sister and I were old enough to be left at home alone, we would go to the grocery store with our parents. We were left in the car while they went into the store to do the weekly shopping. We were not prone to behave well in a store and our parents felt this was the best way to get the job done.

Every so often, one of them would come to the front of the store and look out of the window to check on us.

Once, while we were waiting in the car, I got the urge to go to the bathroom. I stuck my head out of the window and hollered to the top of my voice, "Momma, I gotta Pee!" I hollered not once, but several times, embarrassing my sister. She remedied the situation by rolling the window up on my neck! I still needed to pee but I also needed to breath, so I hushed. Momma checked on us just in time to avoid two accidents.

Sometimes I wonder if the guillotining was really an accident.

Writing On The Bathroom Wall

*N*ormally, I am not one to commit vandalism. I have only written on the bathroom wall one time.

Creative writing has been my passion for years. Even while I was on the road with my husband, I took the time to write. Often, I chose to write when we were between hauls and I could sit in a truck stop diner booth and relax.

The constant vibration of the cab made writing very difficult, to say the least. The thrum of the engine also made it hard to concentrate.

Once while at a stop, (I don't remember where). I went to the ladies room and in the stall scrawled on the wall someone had written:

If I were a dog and you were a flower, I'd lift my leg and give you a shower. The writer in me couldn't resist writing, That's okay, there's just one hitch, if you were a dog you'd be a bitch.

Pray For Paint

In 1983 I had the privilege of teaching kindergarten in a private school. It was a Christian school in the Baptist church we attended.

Part of my job, as a teacher for the five students in my class was to teach them to pray.

I had two four year old's, two five year old's, and one six year old. The six year old had already attended kindergarten in public school but his parents were not satisfied with the rate he was being taught, so they enrolled him in my class.

Our classroom was very small. It was a windowless room at the front door of the church/school.

Almost immediately, construction began on a new classroom wing to accommodate the anticipated growth of the class sizes and the in furniture needs of both the church and the school.

When it was time to paint the walls of what would soon be our new classroom, I asked the students what color they wanted their room. They unanimously chose blue. We began praying daily at the altar for someone to buy or donate their paint color choice for our room.

Several days went by and several prayers went up. Soon after, the Pastor, who was also the Principal of the school announced, someone had donated four gallons of paint. It was a very pretty pastel green. I said to the children, "That's wonderful! Let's go to the altar and thank the Lord for the beautiful green paint we will have on our walls.

Each child took a turn thanking Jesus for the paint. When it came time for five year old Dawn's turn, she prayed, "Dear Jesus, thank you for the green paint, but you know we wanted blue!"

The Kittens Get a Bath

Sammy, the same little boy who painted the porch with mustard, did something else quite comical around the age of three.

The family cat just had five kittens. She chose to give birth in Sammy's closet. He would not leave the family alone. More than a few times, Sammy's mother had to get him out of the closet so the mamma cat could have some peace.

Sammy wanted to know why she did what she did. He was also curious as to why she licked her kittens so much. He did not know that she was washing his scent off her babies whenever he would put them down long enough. Sammy asked his momma why the cat was licking the kittens, and she told him, the mama cat was bathing them. The next time Sammy's mother came to pull him out of the closet, she noticed the mamma cat was foaming at the mouth. She thought the cat was sick with rabies or something.

Instead, she found out that Sammy had poured liquid bubble bath on the kittens.

Potholder Hair

*M*omma never was a beautician. She didn't have the knack for doing hair. She wore her own hair in long braids.

She wrapped the two braids twice around her head and secured them with bobby pins.

My hair was baby-fine until I was seven years old. Momma 'fixed' my hair for me every morning before I went to school.

She would part my hair on both sides and across the crown. Then she secured the tassel with a rubber band.

She then braided the tassel and gathered the ends with a second rubber band. The braid was then looped over and the whole thing was anchored by a coil from the first rubber band. I was teased at school and called "Potholder Hair" by some of the crueler kids. My hair may have looked less than coiffed, but at least it was out of my eyes.

The Lock Washer

*E*veryone has a close brush with death at some point and time in their life. My brush came at the age of two and a half.

My sister and I were playing in the front yard while our mother watched from the kitchen window.

I saw a shiny object in the dirt and as two-year-old's are prone to do, I put it in my mouth.

Momma saw me do it. She was outside in a flash but by the time she reached me I was turning blue. She plunged her finger down my throat and brought out the lock washer I had swallowed.

I thank God that he knew how long my mother's pinkie finger was. I have had other close calls in my life since that time, but I know that Momma's quick thinking and watchful eye is what saved my life that day.

A Child's Sense Of Reasoning

*W*hen my sister's little girl was four years old, she was playing outside one day when a flock of birds came into the yard.

These birds had been making their way down the block visiting each newly mowed lawn and gleaning every available morsel from them as they descended in multitudes, defying anyone who approached them, by simply walking away. There were so many, my niece was literally wading in birds.

Selena tried to catch a bird but was unsuccessful, to say the least. She became frustrated and went inside. She asked her mother to help her catch a bird.

My sister related, when we were young our mother told us we could catch a bird if we put salt on its tail.

Selena ran into her room and got her rusty old birdcage she'd had for her hamster who died about a year earlier. She then went into the kitchen and grabbed the salt shaker from the stove. It was a large shaker with a pitcher-type handle. Out the door she went with the salt and the cage. Soon, she was back in the house crying, "Momma," she said, "I can't get the salt on those bird's tails. They won't stay still!"

My sister replied, "I think that is the idea. I don't think you are supposed to catch them because they are wild." Selena said, "Okay Momma." She went back outside with the salt shaker still in her hand.

"Momma, I put salt on the cat's tail!" Selena squealed excitedly. "It doesn't work on cats, honey," her mother said. "it must work, he's not going anywhere!"

Is It Rodney?

*E*aster was a special time at our house when I was a child. Aunt Jo would always give us the biggest and best Easter baskets. They would be filled with all kinds of goodies.

Once, there was a live baby chick in each one of our baskets. The chicks were dyed pink, blue, and green. Mine was green. It died after only a few days because I handled it too much.

Lois' chick was of a hardier stock. He survived all the torment. She named him Rodney.

Rodney became he cock-of-the-walk in the back yard with seven hens in his harem. He roosted on the large branch four feet up in the oak tree, just a few steps from the back door of our house.

One winter, he got frostbite and his toes froze off. Those seven hens did all his scratching for him from then on.

Rodney disappeared one day and we never knew what became of him. For months after his disappearance, whenever we had chicken for dinner, one of us would ask. "Is it Rodney?"

How I Learned To Count

*E*ach week when Momma did her grocery shopping, she would buy a bag of jelly beans. She picked out all of the black ones because licorice was her favorite.

Momma gave the rest to my sister to share with me. Jeannie would sit on the floor and make two piles of candy, one for herself and one for me.

Somehow her pile always seemed larger than mine. I was only three, but I quickly learned the more jelly beans there were in your pile the bigger your share was.

I don't know if the operative word "equally" was ever used when Momma told my sister to share. However, when I began to balk at her unfairness, the shares did become more equal. I did not know what numbers were, but I could tell by sight if Jeannie had more than I did.

Cookies were less obvious, so I'm sure I was gypped out of many cookies.

It Is Harder To Forget

My favorite teacher was Mrs. Sexton. She was my sixth grade teacher at Glencrest elementary school in Fort Worth, Texas.

I thought she was the best and most talented of all my teachers.

Mrs. Sexton taught music, reading, spelling, and social studies.. We had to go to the other sixth grade teachers for arithmetic and English.

One of the lessons I learned from Mrs. Sexton was, it is harder to forget, than it is to remember. She said, "I will say a number and I want you to forget it."

The number we were given was 1,536. Try to remember something and you may not be able to recall it on demand, but try to forget and you very well may remember it for the rest of your life.

I have remembered that number forever.

Sammy Paints The Porch

*C*hildren are a constant source of humor. Show me a three year old and I'll show you a natural comedian. Kids are funny without even trying to be. Innocence is hilarious.

My friend was very creative and was painting her bathroom window to match her shower curtain, which was a lovely floral design. She had her paints, paintbrushes, and rags all spread out on newspaper on her front porch.

In the course of the project, she smeared a brushful of paint on the porch. The paint was a bright yellow. Rather than admit she had erred, she remarked to Sammy, who was watching the proceedings, "Wouldn't the porch look pretty that color?"

My friend cleaned up the work area and removed the yellow paint from the porch moments before her other children got home from school. That afternoon while the school children were doing homework, Sammy was outside being unusually quiet. My friend went to check on him and found him to be as creative as she. He was busy painting the porch bright yellow. His paint…was a large jar of mustard.

Red Jell-O

*I*t was near Christmas time and Momma had bought my baby sister a beautiful dress to have her picture taken in. The dress was white with tiny red polka-dots. Momma bought a pair of red ruffled panties for my sister to wear with the dress.

Momma dressed the baby and they went to the mall where the photographer's studio was located. They had several pictures taken. Some were of the baby alone, others were of Momma and the baby together. It took quite a while to get the desired results, as my sister was not very helpful. When they finished, they went to the cafeteria to get lunch before returning home.

While choosing their meal, the baby saw a small plate of red Jell-O and exclaimed loudly, "Look Momma, that Jell-O is the same color as my panties." She gleefully lifted her dress so everyone around her could see. Momma's face nearly matched both the dessert and the underwear. When Momma got home, she told us the story with tears of laughter.

Dru's Ballet Oose

*W*hen Sammy's sister was three years old, she was in a dance class. There were about twenty, three and four year old boys and girls in the class. The class was to be a part of a dance recital at the high school one evening.

Dru was still learning to talk and had not mastered all the sounds of the English language. Namely, she could not make the 's' properly. Rather than say a word with an 's' incorrectly by substitution, she would omit the 's' sound altogether. For example, the word soap was pronounced "oap". Sister, became "iter" and so on.

At the recital Dru was supposed to change from her tap shoes to her ballet slippers for the group's second number. Dru returned to the stage in her costume, but with her taps still on.

In her loudest three year old voice she cried, "Momma, I need my ballet oose."

She repeated the request several times. All eyes were on Dru. She squatted on the stage and promptly wet her pants.

How To Muzzle A Pekingese

My husband and I had a Pekingese dog named Tony. The dog went with us every time we were on the road driving long-haul.

We had very little space to store our clothes and such so we often had to wash at the truck stop laundry wherever we happened to be.

Once, I was doing the laundry while my husband was getting caught up on some much needed zzzzz.

Tony was with me. A woman who came into the laundry, began to show signs of being afraid of the dog.

I had been shoving our clothes into a duffle bag. I picked up a pillow case, opened it wide, and told Tony to get in, he walked into the pillow case and laid down. I picked up the duffle bag and the pillow case and left the laundry.

From that point on, whenever I held a pillowcase open for him, Tony would get in.

He would not go into paper or plastic bags, only pillow cases. That's one way to muzzle a Pekingese.

Karen's I's

*W*hen I was teaching in private school, one of my assignments was to teach them to read and print the alphabet.

Each day I would introduce the students to a new letter of the alphabet and show them how the letter was to be written. I would tell them the letter and then tell them the various sounds each letter made.

The first letter we did, was the letter 'I'.

I taught them all the different sounds the letter 'I' makes and we practiced recognizing each sound. I also taught them how to write the letter, which I assumed everyone knew, was a straight line.

The lower case being a shorter version of the same line with a dot over it. However, Karen, chose to do it differently. She made her lower case 'I' just as long as the upper case 'I'. then she flipped her pencil around and erased a small space to create a dot above the line.

When she did this, I knew I had a very creative child in my class and she was going to be a tremendous challenge. She grew up to be a doctor.

The Love Song

*I*n my class of five students, my favorite student was the Pastor's grandson. He was the oldest and the most outspoken.

Since he was ahead of the others in scholastic achievements, he was given assignments that were a little more advanced.

Spelling was the hardest course for him to do in the classroom with everything else that was going on.

I came up with the idea to send him into the other room alone and record the words to the spelling test for him to playback and write the words on his paper.

When I retrieved the tape recorder from him, there was a song on it that went like this:

"There was a teacher named Miss Brown, She is the sweetest teacher around. I love you, I love you, I love you Miss Brown."

There was a deep sigh and then he began to read the text from the book flawlessly.

At that moment, I truly felt I was exercising my calling as a teacher and my students liked and appreciated me for my efforts.

Steeple Chase

*O*ur Pastor was in his study preparing his Sunday Sermon. It was raining that day. The rain was pouring off the roof of the church and splashing so hard against the window, it was difficult for him to concentrate.

He grew weary of trying to read, so he closed his eyes for a moment. Just as his eyelids shut, lightning struck the steeple, making a tremendous noise. It severed the steeple and the wind sent it tumbling several hundred yards down the street with the Pastor chasing after it.

Although the damage to the steeple was minimal, we got really great sermons for several weeks.

There is nothing like a wakeup call directly from the Almighty to make one strive for improvement.

Eewe, Look At That Bug

My cousins who lived in California came to visit us in Texas one summer. We all went to a Lake Camp we had been to the previous year.

The cabins were rustic, dilapidated and miserably hot. Even the bugs came in to escape the heat.

Our cabin had a leaky faucet in the kitchen sink. The moisture drew all manner of tiny wildlife.

The Cicadas were especially noisy, making it difficult to sleep. My cousin, Cindy, got up to get a glass of water. She saw a bug in the sink and pointed to it. She said, "Eewe, a bug!"

I got up to see what she was upset about. She was pointing her index finger millimeters from the biggest scorpion I had ever seen!

She had never seen one and I never wanted to see another one again.

What To Name The Baby

*M*omma was going to have a baby. Here were already three girls. Daddy wanted a son so badly that he would not even discuss a girl's name with Momma.

Momma named the first baby, Daddy named me and Momma was supposed to name Lois but Daddy beat her to it.

This meant that number four was Momma's call. The 'boy' was to be named James Weaver Herriott.

Momma decided that if she was going to get any help from Daddy naming this one, she was going to have to trick him into it somehow.

Jeannie was Betty Jean after Momma and her youngest sister Norma Jean. I was named Renna Jo after my Dad's two sisters. Lois Ann was named for Daddy's two grandmothers, whose names were Lois and Ann. They were running out of possibilities.

When Momma was a young girl, she had three very best friends. They were, Ester Pauline, Ethel Virginia and Grace Lynn. Pauline went by Polly.

When Daddy got home from work one day shortly before the baby was born, Momma met him at the door to announce she had decided on a name if the baby was a girl. She told him she wanted to name her after her three best friends. She said, "I want to name her Polly Ethel Lynn." Instead, they decided on Myra Jannelle, after Momma's doctor Myra, and Janelle after my sister Lois' best friend.

Sleeve Note

*T*his is a story about Staffen Kelly. This one occurred in the late fifties. The health department issued a health warning of a danger of typhoid from the drinking water being contaminated when the river overflowed. Industries were not under such scrutiny as they are today.

The river was quite polluted. Everyone was urged to get a typhoid shot. Especially children and older folks.

The Kelly family had all the children vaccinated including themselves.

The following Sunday, Staffen showed up at church wearing a piece of paper pinned to his sleeve. The paper read: Do not hit…I got a shot.

He knew how boys greeted each other and felt the necessity to post a warning sign. He played the sympathy angle to the hilt that day.

Staffen's Fish

*S*taffen was the son of one of the largest families that attended the same church my family and I did. He was the fifth of six children. There was hardly enough of anything to go around, so Staffen rarely got anything new. If it weren't for hand-me-downs, he might have gone through life naked.

There was also a shortage of toys and sports gear in their household of stairstep siblings.

Once our family and the Kelly's went fishing together. Almost everyone had a cane pole. There were not enough to go around so the younger children were not allowed to fish.

We were on the bank of the river for hours and no one got as much as a nibble. All the non-fishing children were occupying themselves by chasing butterflies as well as each other. However, Staffen was busy with some discarded fishing line he had found.

He also found a shiny safety pin in the glove compartment of his parent's car and fashioned himself a hook.

With the makeshift line and a small branch from a nearby tree, he was soon down to the business of doing decidedly serious fishing. Staffen was the only one who caught a fish that day.

Traffic Control

*W*hen my sister and I were very young, we lived on a country road that was only traveled by those who lived out there and every so often a visitor or two would use that road.

We had a neighbor who lived more than a mile past our house. It seemed like he was always in a hurry as he would drive past us at a high rate of speed as he went up and down that road.

One day, Daddy flagged him down and told him, "If I catch you driving past my house more than ten miles an hour, I'm going to be shooting at a rabbit across the road. Get my meaning?" That man never even stirred the dust when he passed by after that.

Pushing Buttons

My niece, Selena was about three years old the Christmas she had gotten a brightly colored toy cassette player. It was yellow with three buttons, one red, one blue and one green. There were no other moving parts.

My sister and brother-in-law had just gotten their first VCR. They had a time learning to program and operate it. Selena tried to offer her help but was told she was never to touch it.

The neighbor was visiting a few days later and picked up the toy cassette player and began pressing the keys and examining the toy. He muttered, "What a waste, it doesn't do anything."

Selena corrected him by saying, "Yes it does. It lets little children push buttons without getting their tails busted."

The Tar Baby

This is a story my Daddy likes to tell from his childhood. Daddy was twelve years old and he had just re-built himself a bicycle of parts he had earned by helping the scrap collector. He was anxious to try out his 'new' bike.

He went to the neighborhood kid's favorite coasting hill. He had not had a bike in quite a while so did not know the road was closed for resurfacing. He wondered why he was the only kid there. He started down the hill anyway. He realized too late that the road was laden with fresh tar at the foot of the hill. He applied the brakes much too hard and sent himself flying into the still warm goo.

He walked his bike home and had to take a bath in kerosene to remove the tar from his body. He suffered friction burns as well, but they were not as difficult to heal as his wounded pride. Everyone it seemed, had heard about the 'tar baby'.

How Daddy Got His Nickname

$\mathcal{D}$addy has a last name for a first name and a very unusual last name. Most often people failed to pronounce it properly the first few times they tried.

Daddy had an old clunker of a car in a perpetual state of disrepair that he drove to his job every day. The automobile had a faulty battery cable connection he was unaware of. He went to work as usual one day, the battery became drained of power and the car would not start. He had to get a boost from a co-worker.

The co-worker suggested that if Daddy was going to continue to drive salvage yard rejects, he might consider backing into his parking space to avoid difficulty in connecting the jumper cables.

Daddy took the man seriously and for as long as he worked at the hospital, he backed into his space. That was when he acquired the nickname, 'Back up Herriott.'

Daddy continued using that same strategy everywhere he went for as long as he was able to drive, even when he had a brand new car.

Momma Made Fudge…Once

*O*nly one time in my entire childhood do I remember Momma ever making fudge. She got the idea that she would make plenty to share and to have all she wanted so she tripled the recipe.

She made so much that she ran out of containers to put it in. She scurried all over the house trying to find suitable dishes to put her fudge in. She put it in every bowl, pan, tray, and saucer she was able to lay her hands on. She dumped the ice from the ice trays and filled them with fudge. She washed the big glass ashtray and filled it with fudge.

The candy began to cool and she was running out of vessels in which to put it, so she scraped the last of the mixture into the dog's dish.

Everyone, and I do mean everyone had fudge for a very long time.

The Pie-Eating Squirrel

*A*bout twenty years ago my mother worked in a bakery. Every evening she would bring home a box of cakes and pies that were rejected because of some imperfection in their appearance.

There was nothing wrong with the way they tasted. They were all delicious, for a while anyway. After about a month or so of these delightful treats they became less delightful as we grew tired of them.

Momma brought home a half dozen lemon meringue pies one evening and we all moaned at the sight of them.

Angry at our lack of gratitude, she took them out to the freezer that was in the yard (there was no room for the freezer in the house) and sat the pies on top of the freezer and a few on the doghouse.

Later one of us notice a very excited squirrel feasting on the pies. The meringue on his face made him appear rabid. He chattered loudly as he ate. Momma got her camera out and was able to get a picture just as twenty more squirrels arrived to join the party.

Frog Wranglers

I took Biology in the tenth grade. We were tasked to dissect a frog and I was less than thrilled.

I was the kind of kid who would rather play with a frog than gaze upon his entrails.

I spent Sunday afternoon with my girlfriend and we went exploring. We came to a stock pond that was not quite large enough to fish in, but still there was an overturned aluminum boat on the bank.

We decided to go for a boat ride. When we turned the boat over to get inside, we were startled by what seemed like hundreds of frogs, they were everywhere. We spent the rest of our time at the pond catching frogs.

We thought we could make a lot of money selling them to schools to use in the Biology classes. We also thought we'd fry us some frog legs for supper. We fashioned a creel out of a piece of canvas we'd found. We hauled about a hundred frogs back to my friend's house. Of course, her parents made us release them, but for a while we were the best frog wranglers in Texas.

Where Does The Gas Go When The Balloon Dies?

We were sitting in the living room of our parents' house watching the Thanksgiving day parade on television while Momma prepared the multi-course meal.

The announcer would describe each balloon as it came into view. He always told how much helium was used to fill the balloon.

My seven year old nephew asked, "What do they do with all that gas when they are through with it?"

His sister quickly responded, "They release it into the air and all the New Yorkers talk funny for about two weeks."

The Butterfly Collection

*W*hen a man and his wife go long-haul trucking, it is nearly impossible to have a hobby one can enjoy while watching the world through bug guts.

This is when I began to take my writing career seriously. I could only write during the stop overs at various points along our route, because the vibration prevented me from writing in the truck.

Instead, I would sit in the restaurant of the truck stop and write while my husband slept in the sleeper of the truck.

Before I started to ride with him, my husband drove alone. Each time he came home he would bring me some little trinket. So, I began collecting butterflies and trinket boxes.

I collected everything from candles to bookends that were shaped like butterflies. I also collected over thirty assorted hat pins in less than three months.

Once, (out of , I suspect) I noticed that many of the trucks had real butterflies stuck to their grills.

I decided to put my writing on hold for a season and I began a butterfly rescue operation. I started making rounds at truck stops, pulling the defenseless insects from their chrome prisons. Some survived, others didn't.

The ones that didn't survive were taken home to be placed in a butterfly frame. I managed to glean quite a sizable collection that spring. The best part was, I didn't kill a single butterfly while doing it.

Boomerang

$\mathcal{S}$trange behavior is not limited to humans in our family. During my adolescent years, we all joined forces to persuade Daddy to let us have a cat.

Daddy hated cats and it was quite a job just keeping our kitten out of his way until she was old enough to be the mouser Momma claimed her to be.

Once Daddy found she had used his shoe for a sandbox. He took her to work with him and tried to give her away, but there were no takers.

He left her there and five day later, she'd made her way back home.

I do not recall what we named her originally, but from that day on, we called her Boomerang.

Daddy had cause to carry her off two more times. Both times, she found her way back to us.

The last time it took her nine months to make her way back home with a litter of kittens in tow.

We kept Boomerang and her kittens. When the kittens were old enough, we gave them away to our school friends.

Boomerang was never evicted again and she lived to be a ripe old age.

The Pants Eating Bike

My niece, Lori was nine years old. She had just gotten a brand new bike for Christmas. She got it while staying at my parent's house.

They lived in a gated community with lots of paved roads, hills and curves, making bike riding a lot of fun for any kid.

Me and my sister Myra and my nephew Lori's brother went bike riding. I put the dog in the wire basket on the handlebars of the bike I was riding. I told the other three kids not to get too far ahead of me and to be careful on the hills.

There was very little traffic and there were multiple signs at every intersection.

It began to rain. The rain was warm and felt good on our sundrenched bodies. Lori had a problem though. She was wearing a tee shirt. The more the rain penetrated the tee shirt, the more you could see through it. Lori, was very modest and the thought of anyone seeing her in that state was uncomfortable for her.

She raced home ahead of us and we lagged behind until it started to thunder, We took the short cut and made it home ahead of Lori.

We thought she may have stopped to take shelter under an awning or pavilion until the storm passed. However, we found out later, that was not the case.

An hour later, Lori still had not shown up. Just as we'd gotten back on our bikes, we spotted Lori coming up the road. She was walking along side of the bike. There was a large rag of some kind hanging from the bike and dragging along the ground. The rag turned out to be Lori's pants. The leg of her jeans had become entangled in her bike chain and she was unable to free herself. So she removed her britches and walked home in her wet see-through shirt and underpants.

She took the long way home so no one would see her. She was wet from the rain, cold from the wind and red-faced from embarrassment.

The Volkswagen Sisters

*A*s my sisters and I got older we also got larger. The four of us together weighed over seven hundred pounds.

My parents lived in a gated community in east Texas. The gate was controlled by a key each property owner had Guests would have to be met at the gate to be let in. There was a panel in the road to open the exit gate when a car rolled over it.

My sisters and I went to the gate area to let my Aunt Jo and Grandma in who were coming from San Antonio.

We saw a Volkswagen car drive up and the gate opened. We thought if it could open the gate, so could we if we pulled our weight.

The three of us began jumping on that panel, having a good time when the security guard crashed our party and sent us home.

Aunt Jo arrived in the nick of time, so we rode back to the house with her.

The Alamo Conspiracy

My sisters and I were strongly discouraged against lying. Momma could do it, but we couldn't. "Do as I say, not as I do," was her pat answer anytime the truth was in question.

Having an aunt living in San Antonio was a guarantee of frequent visits to the Alamo.

My sister, Jeannie and I once concocted an idea to have a push fight at the water fountain near the front entrance. We did this so we could tell our friends that we had a relative who fought at the Alamo without lying.

The Stockyard Incident

I have an abnormal fear of getting lost. I do not enjoy going to large people places like amusement parks and shopping malls with a group of people I have to keep up with.

I have a better time if I designate a place to meet them, then go off on my own. I attribute this phobia to having gotten lost when I was five years old while my family and I were at the Fat Stock Show in Fort Worth.

Somehow I got separated from my folks. I must have gotten sidetracked by a Billy goat or something.

Anyway, when I realized I was alone, I became hysterical. A man from the stocks show commission took me to a room where the auctioneers make their calls. He got on the P.A. system and described me, then gave me a ballpoint pen to hush my crying.

When Jeannie saw I was eating an ice cream cone she said, "I want one, too."

My reply to that request was, "If you want one, you go get lost."

The ice cream soon disappeared but I kept the ballpoint pen as it was the Stock Show's very first year.

The Alligator Pit

*I*n the fearful days of the cold war when President Kennedy was in the white house and Fidel Castro was our country's biggest threat to a peaceful existence Daddy decided to build a fall-out shelter in our back yard.

He went to the hardware store and bought a shovel, a skein of twine and a pack of wooden stakes.

He carefully measured the area where he planned to dig our safe haven. It would be a twenty foot square fifty feet from our back door. He planned to reinforce it with cinder block and cement.

He dug until the pit was two feet deep all the way. By the time this was done, the crisis was settled and the threat was ended. It rained for four days. The pit filled with water.

To keep us out of it, Momma told us that an alligator lived in it. We spent hours chunking stuff at that imaginary reptile.

When one of the puppies fell in, we were in sheer panic. Momma waded in and got him. She was busted in her lie and we had a nice swimming pool.

Miracle At The Mall

*W*hen strange things happen that turn out to be good, I call them miracles. There is one miracle I want to always remember.

Baby sister was barely two years old. We had all gone to the mall to buy school clothes and supplies. Daddy was carrying our respective bags of new clothes.

We all had been walking for what seemed like hours. After shopping, we walked outside of the mall. We were instructed to sit on the bench while Daddy searched for the car. He zig zagged the parking lot with a thirty pound child in his arms.

It was August and the word hot, was an understatement. Daddy became weary, irritated, and angry that he could not find our vehicle.

He sat the baby down on the hood of a car to rest and try to get his bearings. The baby began to pound on the hood of the car with her tiny hand. "Hot tis, hot tis Daddy," she said. Daddy thought she was saying the hood of the car was hot so he picked her up. "We car, we car, Daddy." Sure enough Daddy had sat her down on his own car!

Little Girl Last

My sister, Lois is almost 4 years younger than I am. That made me the middle child for 12 long years. Then I became the middle child of four children.

I was so well rehearsed in the roll of middle child, I did not give it up just because my parents had a fourth child.

I had a habit of sabotaging my own happiness by self-inflicted martyrdom. I would wait in silence for my turn. If the game was over before I got my turn, I would celebrate by throwing myself a pity-party. After a few episodes of this, it became clear a parental decree was needed that we would take turns in alphabetical order by first name. There was Carrol, Linda, Jeannie, and Jo…wait a minute, I was still last! I insisted we do it by age rather than by name. There was Carrol, Jeannie, Linda, and Jo….Wait, how about shoe size?

Broken Leg

My husband and I had only been married two years when he bought me a canary for my birthday. We named him Romeo. He was a sweet little companion to enjoy when my husband was working off shore in South Louisiana.

One niece was living with us at the time and she was always asking to be allowed to get the bird out to play with him.

My sister who was the same age as my niece was visiting us. The girls were in the back room where the bird was kept safe from the cat.

Suddenly the two young ladies rushed into the living room and sat down on the sofa. They remained unusually quiet.

Later we discovered that Romeo's leg was broken. The girls tearfully fessed up. We repaired the bird's leg with a toothpick and an adhesive bandage. The leg mended. The girls cried themselves to sleep that night.

The Grasshopper Graveyard

*C*ruelty to animals was greatly discouraged in our home, but cruelty to insects was not listed in this category. To the insect community, we were death on tricycles.

My uncle had just passed away and I had my first encounter of the harsh reality with the passing of life. I first saw human remains and my first up close look at a cemetery. I was impressed.

It was not a morbid fascination, rather it was an aesthetic one. I liked the neat rows of markers and the lovely flowers. I liked the soft organ music and the monotoned eulogy.

This reverent atmosphere gave me a sense of the presence of God.

For days after, I played funeral with grasshoppers. I buried them in rows, making little crosses out of matches and headstones out of dominoes. I place a single honeysuckle flower on each grave.

Catching the grasshoppers was easy. There were so many, one didn't even need a net. Even the minister refused to accept payment for his part.

It was after Wednesday night prayer meeting at the church and since he was already there….

We left Texas that night to make our home in Thibodaux, Louisiana. This was in 1967. Most of our friends had divorced and remarried, some had remarried several times. We have stuck it out because good friends are hard to find. Making them the 'Deceased' was the hard part.

My graveyard was the eternal resting place for about thirty-three headless grasshoppers!

The Purloined Pickles

My late husband, Don has loved dill pickles for as long as I have known him. He likes the big sour ones that drip vinegar down your arm when you bite into it.

My mother-in-law, Alice bought a gallon jar of pickles to take to a church picnic. She told Don not to eat all those pickles before she could take them to the function.

However, he wore her down, begging for a pickle as soon as he spied them in the refrigerator. She conceded and he got a pickle.

Come pickle serving time, there was only one pickle left in the jar. Don's defense was, "You said, don't eat all the pickles." Later he wished he hadn't.

The Outhouse

*T*here are happenings in my
childhood, that simply must be told. I'll tell
it now while I still can, before I grow too
old.

When I was about five years old,
we had two paths outback
One path lead us to the well
And one to a rundown shack.

Outhouses were common then
we were glad we had one,
It was falling down and visits were never
any fun.

We'd hurry back inside
especially at night.
 We'd go to the outhouse in pairs
So one could hold the light.
My friend and I were in there
When the bull broke from the pen.
He headed straight for that shack
I nearly jumped out of my skin

I tried to pull my britches up,
but the bull gave me no chance.

So we quickly left the outhouse
Without my underpants.
I left them where I dropped them
right there on the floor.
I was in such a hurry to get out of there, I
think I broke the door.

We reached the safety of the house
And looked back in time to see
A big pile of rubble where the
Outhouse used to be.

I'm still here to tell this tale,
Intact, body and soul.
But I believe I owe my life to
one strategically placed knothole.

On Being An Un-Twin

My older sister was only seventeen and a half months old when I was born. The closeness of our births compelled Momma to regard us as twins to a certain extent.

She dressed us alike and did our hair alike and often dressed us alike except for the color. if she could not afford two of any one item, she would forgo the purchase.

One Easter, I was dressed in pink and my sister was dressed in blue. The next year it would be reversed. We got identical shoes, same size and everything.

Momma would mark mine with O's which were at the right toe and the left heel. My sister's shoes were marked the same way with the X's. This served a dual purpose. It identified the owner of the shoes and taught us left from right. Momma was strange, but smart.

I remember when Momma took me and my older sister Jeannie to enroll us in school at the brand new Glen Park Elementary

School. She took the short cuts as she walked us to school, so we could learn the way and walking home would be quicker.

When we got to school, all was fine until we got inside. Momma had each of us by the hand walking us to our new classrooms.

I was walked to my class first and Jeannie, second.

The cleaning lady spotted us and declared, "Lawdy, mussy, here come anodder one." She had been counting sets of twins. Another incident of mistaken identity gone uncorrected.

The Ugly Duckling Club

*W*hen I was in high school, I was not what one would call one of the beautiful people. Actually, I was quite homely. I was five feet eight inches tall and weighed ninety-eight boney, shapeless pounds.

I was a stick with hair, and every day was a bad hair day.

I was not a very social being either. I had a few friends who I really liked and several superficial friendships.

I would not say I'd come in dead last in a Miss Popularity contest, but I would certainly be a runner-up for most shy.

I suffered from low self-esteem even before it was a common ailment. My remedy for my unpopular status, was to befriend the girls who were even less attractive than I, making myself the best looking one of our group.

We were the target of affection for the boys in the counter group, who dated the pretty girl's rejects.

I learned, just because one is not physically attractive, does not mean one is not attractive. In my senior year, I went to the ROTC Cotillion and the Homecoming game and dance with my boyfriend. We went steady for nine months. He was a junior and several months younger than I, but we were very fond of each other.

When he told me, he wanted to make the Army his career, we broke up because I didn't want to be a military wife.

Three years later, he was killed in action in Viet Nam.

Where The Devil Comes Up

$\mathcal{M}$omma told us scary things, too. She told me and my sisters that manholes in the street is where the devil came up to eat little girls.

I think she said this, to make sure we stayed away from dangerous places like sewers and drainage pipes. Her strategy didn't work, though.

We made a playhouse out of cardboard boxes in the maze of a huge network of newly installed sewer pipes in the park about half a mile from our house.

The park was only three blocks away, but the playhouse was deep into the tunnels. We marked the walls with chalk to find our way out. Our only source of light was the manhole from which we removed the cover on the street above us. I don't think Momma ever knew we did that. If she knew, she never said anything.

Old What's His Name

*O*ur family had gone to Mangum, Oklahoma to visit our Great Grandparents. Granddaddy Earnest wanted to show us the sights in and around his homeplace, where he'd lived most of his life.

Geronimo had died recently and was buried not too far from where Granddaddy grew up, and so we were able to visit Geronimo's grave.

Granddaddy said, "If you walk around Geronimo's grave three times and ask him, What are you doing? He'll say nothing." To our embarrassment, we found out that was true.

Months later, my sister and I were asleep in the bed we shared when I sat up, shook her shoulder and asked, "Jeannie, what was that Indian's name?" Her curt reply was, "Geronimo, now go back to sleep."

To this day, I still do not know how she knew the correct answer.

Boyfriend, to Boyfriend, to Best Friend

My late husband, Donald was my older sister's boyfriend and ultimately her fiancé during our teenage years. They started going steady when they were fourteen. By the time she was sixteen, they had agreed to marry when she finished school and he returned from the service.

While he was gone, she met someone else and broke off her engagement to Donald. When he returned home from the service, he wanted to go out but all the girls he knew from our circle of friends were going with someone, so he asked me. I do not care to know how many he asked before me, but I know I was not the first.

We went out with friends to the circus. We had a really good time. We had a total of four dates then we got married. The dates were several weeks apart as Don was working in the oilfield in Louisiana at the time.

Our wedding cost $56. That included the dress, veil, shoes and wedding cake.

What's In A Name?

*W*ith a family name like Herriott, we were often teased by our schoolmates. We had to endure being called "Hairy It, Her Riot" and other names not associated with our name, just because our surname lends itself so easily to ridicule.

Momma always said, if they did not like us, they would not tease us. What a lie that was! Those kids did not like us because we were the new kids and they were so into cliques. No one wanted to be bothered with the new girls.

I was friendly to everyone. Even the outsiders shunned me for a while until I discovered a common thread that drew us together. Somehow, we realized all the outsiders had green eyes.

The outsiders became the emerald club. Only green eyed people were allowed to be a part of our now elite group. The insiders began ejecting green eyed kids from their groups. Hence, no more cliques!

The Phone Call

My nephew, Damon was about ten years old when he and his friends went to the mall's toy store. They were totally unaware that they were being watched by the manager as well as the store's surveillance cameras.

The manager of the store watched as my nephew shook his head in a negative gesture, folded his arms and walked away from his friends. He went to a corner of the store and stood there facing the corner until his friends were approached by security. They had taken some small die cast cars and put them under their jackets. My nephew had no part in the theft. He held on to his desire to refrain from stealing.

My sister got a phone call from the store manager that went something like this: "I am used to calling parents to tell them that their child is in trouble for shoplifting in my store. But I just want to let you know what your one did." Then he proceeded to tell her what happened. Sometimes good parenting pays off!

Curtain Circus

The old house we lived in had no door on the larger of the two bedrooms. My parents put my sisters and I in the smaller room and took the other room.

Daddy took the closet door off the closet and placed it on the bedroom door. Momma thought the open closet was an accident waiting to happen with three toddlers in the house, so she made some curtains out of an old Chanelle bedspread. She secured the dowel in the doorway and succeeded in hiding the attractive danger zone.

I do not remember how my sister and I figured out how to swing on that curtain, but we did. We pretended we were circus performers and the closet was the big top. We used the dowel rod for a trapeze. A sound spanking was the consequences for "bringing the house down." The circus never visited our home again.

Cactus Dip

$\mathcal{F}$or my husband's 42nd birthday I bought him a beautiful yellow cockatiel bird. He named him Cactus.

Cactus was hand raised so it was a common practice of ours to allow him to leave his cage on occasion. We simply opened the door to the cage and he would venture out at his leisure.

We always turned the ceiling fan off before we opened the cage door. We also kept cactus' wings clipped to be on the safe side.

Once Don had fried some fish in a big Dutch oven on top of the stove. The cooker was full of cooking oil. It was being allowed to cool down to room temperature before it was to be drained and stored for further use.

I opened the cage to let cactus stretch his wings. I did not realize it had been a while since we clipped his wings. He flew directly into the kitchen and landed squarely into that vat of oil.

It was no longer hot enough to burn him, but it did give him a thick coat of oil. I could only think of all the poor birds that lost their lives due to the oil spills in the gulf. I could not bear for the bird I had grown to love to perish in that manner. I grabbed the bird and the dish soap. I gave that bird the first and only bubble bath he ever had.

I saved his life with my quick response to his dilemma. He lived but he lost every feather he had. He looked like a hatchling buzzard for about two weeks. When his feathers grew back, he was not as yellow as he had been. There was white mixed in with the yellow.

Cactus never talked. Do you suppose it is because he never quite forgave me for that bath?

We Get The Chicken Pox

*M*y sister, Jeannie, and I got the Chicken Pox at the same time. Jeannie, was in the first grade at Forest Hills elementary school. The majority of her class had already had the Chicken Pox. She played in the sand box with the only kid in her class who was contagious.

She then brought the virus home. We broke out in blisters about two hours apart. Momma warned us repeatedly not to scratch our blisters even though they itched fiercely. She told us if we scratched our blisters, we would get ugly scars. With Momma's track record for the truth, we didn't scratch our blisters: We scratched our sister's blisters.

The Horse Got My Bottle

I believe this might classify, as one of Momma's best lies. When it came time to wean me from my bottle, she told me that the horse got my bottle.

There was a sweet old swayback mare that lived in the pasture behind our property on route seven in rural Fort Worth.

That old horse had seen better days and was simply living out her remaining years as a companion to the boy who owned her. She was as gentle as rain and her wildest desire was to be fed a sugar cube occasionally.

My older sister was still prone to take a bottle for napping purposes only, you understand? I also took a bottle, but I wanted mine all the time and I was very fond of it. We threw rocks unmercifully at that poor old horse. I don't think we hit her. But I know we saw less of her after that.

Fannie And The Butane Tank

My parents friends, Buddy and Fanny Gibson lived way out in the country. They used butane for heating and cooking. There was a huge tank sitting about ten yards from the back door of the house. It was painted silver. The tank got hot in the summer afternoons. Too hot to touch comfortably.

The tank stood about six feet off the ground on a scaffold-like stand. This made the total height about eleven feet tall.

Fannie was sweeping the dirt out the back door one hot afternoon when she saw a snake she swore was ten feet long. (No one else saw it but her).

When her husband got home from work that day, he found Fannie perched on top of that hot butane tank. Fannie, who stood all of four feet three inches tall, doesn't know how in the world she was able to get up there!

Selling The Baby

My baby sister, Myra was only nine months old when we got the idea to sell her. We were not serious, of course. But we had fun offering her to the customers who came to the produce stand. If anyone asked how much we wanted for her, we told them she could be sold for a million dollars a pound and they should buy her while her weight was down.

We would plop her on the scales we used to weigh the produce to see what the going price would be. She would have been worth nine million at birth. We decided to keep her. I guess I will have to make my fortune writing books.

Pet Names

*C*hoosing a name for a pet is not always an easy task. Some pets earn their names by their looks or behavior. We were never one to name a pet any traditional names. No Fido ever graced our backyard.

No Bowser, Fluffy, or Rex, either. We had dogs named Toby, Timex, Queenie, Griswold, King, Leastest, Bruiser, Penny, Chinky Bear, Billy, Jake, Timi Tu, Sparkle, Trinket, Tuffy and Taffy, D.J. and Lance.

We had cats named, Marble, Cisero, Cessna, Mazda, and one we didn't have long enough to name. It escaped as soon as we got it home and we never saw it again.

The best dog we ever had was a Pekingese named Tony. Once we lived next door to a family named Toney and would you believe it? Their dog was named Brown E.

Mr. Thompson's Bell

I was in the eleventh grade in High School in 1965. My Math teacher was Mr. Guy Thompson. He was a very good teacher and he was liked by all his students. Even those like me who hated Math, liked Mr. Thompson.

Mr. Thompson had a bell on his desk. He rang that bell to call class to attention and to signal the end of a test.

He never made any comments about the bell, how he got it, or from whom. His fifth period class assumed another class had gotten it for him years before or that he had bought it for himself. Neither assumption was true.

The fifth period class took that bell to have it engraved with a sentiment from them to Mr. Thompson as a gesture of affection. It was missing from his desk for about two weeks.

As the days wore on without the bell being returned, we all began to notice

Mr. Thompson's demeanor change. He was not as cheerful as he usually was. He was temperamental and rather curt to his students. Finally he breached the issue of the missing bell.

"I will hold no one to blame if my bell is returned within the next two days." He said to each of his classes. There was a sadness in his voice that was unmistakable. His heart was broken.

The fifth period class got the bell back from the engraver just in time. They had it gift wrapped and presented it to him as a token of their appreciation on the last day of school.

When Mr. Thompson opened that package and discovered his bell, he was delighted. But when he saw it had been engraved, he burst into tears. The students thought at first he was overjoyed. But, to him it was ruined because it appeared as though the bell was a gift from his students and not from his dying father. "You kids have ruined my bell." He shouted. "How could you be so cruel?"

"This was my father's bell. He used it in the one room schoolhouse he taught in when he was a teacher in the 1890's in Virginia."

"I was the only one of his thirteen children to follow in his footsteps to become a teacher, so he gave this bell to me on his deathbed. It meant more to me than anything I owned."

When the school bell rang for the last time that year, there were twenty seven very sad students offering up apologies to a very fine teacher and giving him hugs in genuine love.

He was truly a remarkable teacher and a fine individual. I am glad I was in his fourth period class that year.

.

The Kiss Of Life

My Pekingese dog was about to deliver her first litter. She was only six months old, so she was still very much a puppy herself.

She was really too young to be having puppies, but I was looking forward to helping her be a good mother, and also to getting some extra money when I sold the puppies.

When the time came for her to deliver she was acting as though she had not a clue as to what was happening to her. When the first puppy emerged she tried to run from it. I calmed her down with soft words and took the puppy. I cut the cord and showed the puppy to its mother. Then I put the new born baby in a warm towel and waited for the next one to arrive.

The second puppy came about ten minutes after the first one. All was right and I repeated the procedure.

When the third pup started its emergence he came hind feet first. By this time the mother dog had caught on that she was supposed to lick the pups clean as they were born. She was cleaning the wrong end. The puppy was writhing in an attempt to get a breath.

I took the puppy as I had the others and quickly scrubbed his face. I placed my mouth over his entire head and blew life into him. Out of that litter, he was the only survivor. We named him Tony and he was our most beloved pet for almost fifteen years.

The Kiss Of Death

My husband and I were house parents at a residential care facility for boys and girls in Southern North Carolina a few years back. We had the challenge of the charge of twelve very lively young boys. The boys loved to play pranks.

I was their favorite target. I think it was because I was so unpredictable. One of the boys caught a tree frog one night. Some of the guys suggested that they torment me with it, thinking I was afraid of tiny, wet, slimy, amphibians.

I astonished them by asking to hold the frog and then I appalled them by kissing it. I kissed the cute little frog right on its mouth. I said, "Well, you must not be a prince." At that point I let the frog go.

The boys caught him again and put him in a box. The next morning we discovered the frog was dead! For several days after that I threatened to kiss anyone who misbehaved!!

Getting Flashed

The year I was five years old my parents bought a new two-bedroom house on Ollie Street in Fort Worth, TX. There was another house to the North and several houses across the street but nothing behind our house or to the South. The field behind us was simply acres of Johnson Grass.

It was not long until the property next door was purchased by Dr. Brooks. He had his office built on the site. This was not too bad as we then had a safe place to ride our bikes when the office was closed. There was even a security light making it possible to ride after dark. We had to be in the house every evening by seven. During the fall and winter months it was dark by six.

The problem arose when the property behind us was used to build a Safeway grocery store. This in itself was not a problem but the store sign that flashed in through our bedroom window was. The flashing sign sent eerie shadows across my bed feeding my already vivid imagination. I saw all kinds of creatures in the lights and shadows of the room. The sign flashed light green, dark green, pink and yellow. With each color, new terrors lurked in the darkness to rob me of my nightly rest.

I love the fact that I have a good imagination but I still hate that sign. I did not sleep well the entire five years we lived at 5174 Ollie Street. After we moved, Dr. Brooks bought the house, had it razed and made a parking lot. No one else ever had to endure that sign.

If It Folds…Pin It On The Baby

*M*omma did not always have a washing machine. Often, she had to wash our clothes in a wash tub in the backyard. It was difficult but Momma never complained. All our clothes got washed every Saturday. The baby's diapers were washed daily except when the weather was cold or it was raining. In January of 1952, it rained for five days straight. It was bitter cold and impossible to be outdoors for long. Leastwise not long enough to wash clothes. Needless to say, the baby ran out of what few diapers she had. Momma had to improvise. She pinned feed sacks, dish cloths, pillow cases and anything else that could be folded into the shape of a diaper. Daddy went ballistic though when she used one of his tee-shirts.

Three days later Momma got her first electric washer. Momma said, years later, if she had known that was all it took to get a washing machine, she would have put a shirt on the baby's bottom the day she was born. Momma's complaints were always retrospective that way.

El Spinachio

My sister's little girl loved spinach. Even as a toddler she preferred it to corn or carrots. She always ate her spinach even if she had other food on her plate.

Once she was sitting in her high chair enjoying her meal which consisted of a fried chicken leg, French fries, and of course, spinach. My sister dropped her fork so she moved the high chair toward the wall so she could reach the utensil.

Lois neglected to put the baby's chair back in its usual place. The next thing we saw was Lori Lynne painting an abstract on the wall with-what else? Spinach!

Not Over Here!

My ineptness at any kind of sports, cannot be over emphasized. There does not exist a sport in which I excel. I suck equally at them all. Eye/hand co-ordination is not a trait I have the pleasure of possessing. The ability to judge distance, depth, speed, and the laws of physics are necessary for so many games and sports, one such game is pool.

I once played pool with my boyfriend, (who later became my husband). We were on one of the few dates we had before we got married. It was my turn to shoot. Don had scattered the balls well on the break and sunk the two ball. He informed me, I was to concentrate on the striped balls. I was not to aim at, or hit the solids in any way. Also, he said I was to say which hole I was aiming for and with what ball.

I scratched several turns and there were now fewer balls to avoid, so I exclaimed with confidence, "Three ball, side pocket." Echoing the same tone and verbiage I'd heard him use.

I took careful aim and hit the three ball with the cue stick. It jumped the bank of the table, landed on the next table, and went in the side pocket! One of the players on that table growled at me, "Not over here!"

Being the gracious gentleman that he was, Don allowed me to count that shot as a good one because I did call it correctly.

Since I do not enjoy endangering the lives of others, I leave the sports to the sports-minded and I stick to what I do best, which is telling these stories.

Lies I told Momma

I was a child that was not afraid to bend the truth whenever I thought it would serve me well. I was what some would call a chronic liar. I lied to make myself appear more interesting. I lied to avoid getting into trouble.

This always backfired because I got into more trouble for the lies than the original misdeed. I lied to get my sisters into trouble. I lied to get things I desired but would not ordinarily get. One lie of this genre, was to tell my Momma I was going to be a clown in the school play and I needed a clown costume.

My Momma's friend, Pauline's son had a clown suit so Momma borrowed it for me. It hung in my closet for a month before I could come up with a lie to get me out of the first lie. I told Momma the play had been cancelled because the kid who was supposed to be the ringmaster got laryngitis. The clown suit was returned to the lender. It took me years to realize, lies hurt the liar as well as the one you lied to, lied on, or lied about.

Ill-fitting Boots

My daddy always had a habit of putting small objects into larger ones for safe keeping. His room was always so cluttered, it was impossible to keep up with items such as combs or his ever present pocket knives. Daddy had a pocket knife at his disposal at all times. He would use a knife to cut the string binding of his Sunday paper and then he'd casually close it and slip it into a safe place.

After he read his paper, he got up and put on his boots to go walk off the area he planned to put a new storage building. We walked almost every inch of his ten acres with a pocket knife in his boot!

When he returned to the house, he started to complain that his favorite boots no longer fit. He was all set to buy himself a new pair when he accidentally turned one upside down and the knife fell out. He was embarrassed but at the same time, relieved.

The Jackhammer

*M*y husband and I were on our honeymoon. It really wasn't a formal honeymoon. It was more like an errand to New Orleans. Don had to change his W-4 to include me as an exemption for tax purposes.

I had never been to New Orleans. I had never been away from my family. Don was my family now and I clung to him fiercely. I was afraid of getting lost from him in that place and never finding him again.

The buildings were so tall they blocked out the sunlight for most of the day. We were taking a tour of the city when we entered an area where construction of a new parking garage was going on . There were workmen everywhere. Some were on scaffolds, some were in manholes, some were in bucket trucks high in the air.

The one I will never forget was using a jackhammer on the sidewalk we were walking on. Just as we approached, he let it rip. The noise scared me so badly that I christened the new construction a year prematurely. Don't ever ask my husband what I did on my honeymoon!

Damon Hears Music

$\mathcal{M}$y nephew, Damon was about four years old. He and his sister were spending the week with my parents so they could take the children to Vacation Bible School at the church where my folks attended and my mother taught a class of seven-year-olds.

As usual, Damon got to Grandma's without his good shoes. His grandma decided to take him to get a new pair of sneakers at the local department store. While there, Damon kept begging to be allowed to visit the toy department. My mother repeatedly told him, "No."

Momma looked away for an instant and the boy was gone. Momma, knowing where he was headed, went on with her shopping. When she finished, she went to the toy department to find Damon.

She called his name as she approached the toy isle. She put a little anger in her voice so he would know she disapproved of his disappearance. Momma noticed all of the toys that were designed to play music were in full operation. A cacophony of everything from "Row, row, row your boat," to "Pop goes the weasel," was plinking out their tune on about twenty different toys.

"Damon, come here! Didn't you hear me calling you?" Momma said. Damon answered in his sweet voice and with his 'Ain't I cute' grin. "How could I, with all this music in my head?"

Feeling Flushed

I remember as a child, going with my daddy to Sycamore Park in Fort Worth to watch him play baseball.

There was lots to do at the park and it was a much safer time back then. My sisters and I often played on the swings, slides and merry-go-round while Daddy was busy swatting baseballs. There was a multi stall restroom near the sandbox. It boasted a new feature for the era. It had toilets that flushed automatically whenever the user stood up. This was supposed to be the latest new-fangled invention to promote a more sanitary facility.

My little sister, Lois was unaware of this new concept the first time she went with us. She went into the restroom by herself. My older sister and I kept on playing but listened for her to call for help as she always needed help with the toilet paper at that time in her young life.

Time passed and there was no call from Lois. More time passed, still not a sound.

Finally, we got up to go check on her. There she was in the second stall. She was perched on the seat with both feet, afraid to get down.

She screamed that the monster in the hole was trying to suck her down. She was too light to hold the seat down sufficiently to keep the toilet from flushing.

The swirling water, the noise and her imagination had made a trembling wreck of the child. I am convinced some of Momma's lies played a part in the terror my sister endured that day in 1955.

The House Does A Strip Tease

*M*y younger sister, Lois and her husband bought a new house. There were only about ten houses in the subdivision where they moved in their three bedroom home in Everman, Texas.

There were several more homes to be built and sold to young families of a certain income bracket. This meant there would be lots of children for their children to play with and lots of young couples as potential friends. It appeared to be ideal.

One day they had one of those West Texas gully washer rainstorms. It rained fast and hard. The ground was slick because the grass had not had time to germinate on the lawns of the occupied houses. My sister went out to get her morning paper the day after deluge. When she turned to go back into her house, her jaw dropped to her chest. The brick that had graced the front of her house was laying on the ground. It appeared, the brick and mortar, peeled right off the house in a single slice.

It turned out that the problem stemmed from the use of too much water in the mortar. Most of it dissolved in the storm, causing the bricks to fall off.

Hers was not the only house to shed its façade. Some of the near-ready homes had the same problem.

The contractors returned to replace the brick on the first dry day after the storm. I guess things like this are only funny if it doesn't happen to you.

Pig Pile

*A*s most families do at holiday time, ours always collected at a host's house for the traditional Gobble and grunt fest. We gathered at the appointed home as early as possible so we could exchange pictures, gossip and gospel. We often shared an entire year's worth of information as that was the last encounter we had with some of those folks that were there.

After the polite exchange and the oohing and ahhhing over the newest addition to the clan we would all try to find a place at the table and enjoy the feast that was so lovingly prepared by the hapless hostess of the year.

All the older adults played canasta after the meal. The children would watch TV or weather permitting, we would go for a walk. Sometimes we would go to the movies if one was close by. But by far, my favorite thing to do was 'Pig Pile.'

Having sufficiently gorged ourselves, we would begin to feel sleepy. There were never enough beds in the house to accommodate the number of 'pigs' so we would pile on the floor of an out of the way room to take a nap. This became as much a tradition as pumpkin pie for dessert. Some of us looked forward to this time of closeness.

We would talk to one another until the last 'piggy' fell asleep. Ooh! I get a warm fuzzy just thinking about those times. Sadly, they are gone forever.

Debbie's Goozle

We referred to a person's throat as his goozle. My niece had never heard of this reference to that part of the anatomy.

Once, when she had a sore throat, I made the remark, she had a sore Goozle.

She was only five and very bright for her age. I do not know if it was her sense of humor or her innocent youthful mind that made her think I was talking about a goose, when she said, "Aunt Jo, if I had a goozle in my throat, I'd be spitting feathers."

The Hobo's Trail of Handouts

*W*hen I was about five years old, my family lived across the street from the railroad tracks. There were four sets of tracks and they led in every direction.

We were far enough away from the main station that it was a good safe place for the hobos to get on and off the train, undetected.

The hobos would ride the boxcars of the train to wherever they needed to go and by doing so, avoided having to pay train fare. Often the hobos were homeless and rode the rails to keep moving to find shelter and food wherever they could.

Once, I remember a hobo came to our house late one day and knocked on our back door. He was dirty, smelly, and unshaven. His hair looked like it had not been combed or cut in months, and he was hungry.

He asked my mother if she could spare a plate of food. He did not ask for money or anything else, he just wanted something to eat. Momma left him standing at the door in his tattered clothing and his worn out shoes for a few minutes.

Soon she came back to the door with a can of Pork 'n' Beans and a plastic spoon. She handed it to the man and said she was sorry that was all she had.

The man thanked her and went back to the tracks eating the beans as he walked. The next day another hobo showed up at our door. Momma gave him a can of beans, too. Another hungry hobo, then another came to our back door for a can of beans. Momma knew the first man had long since left the area, but still the boxcar riders came to our house for nourishment. They all seemed to know what to ask for and who to ask for the prized can of pork 'n' beans. Somehow the message was being sent out that the lady at 2705 St. Louis Street was kind enough to give food to the hobos.

This went on so long, that Momma started buying pork 'n' beans by the case especially for the hobos.

One day, we noticed a big white X marked on the side walk in front of our house. Daddy washed it off with the garden hose. No hobos came that day. None came the next day either. Daddy realized that the 'X' was a signal to the hobos that food was available there. Daddy bought a box of chalk and marked the 'X' again, the hobos returned.

You see, most of the hobos were wearing tattered military uniforms. They were soldiers trying to get home to their families after the war, and that was our way of helping them.

Punchin' Judy

*W*hen Lois was a little over two there was a doll on the market at Christmas time that was made of celluloid and cloth that resembled Humpty Dumpty, Lois named her Judy.

The face was brightly colored with wide eyes and red lovely lips. It was rather roly poly and had a pair of patent leather shoes that could be removed.

I was tossing the doll in the air and catching it, when I caught it with too much force and put a dent in its lovely face. Lois was watching me so I laughed to keep her from becoming upset. She laughed, too. I did it again on purpose. She laughed again. I doubled my fist and assaulted the doll with a blow to the cheek. It dented and Lois laughed. Soon I was punching dents in the doll as the laughter swelled from the crib.

Momma came to investigate the situation to find me hitting the doll for a loop. She was not pleased with me, to say the least.

The doll was destroyed because the dents could not be taken out.

Babies do not make good comedy critics is the lesson I learned at the tender age of four.

Baby Cuts Her Hair

My sister, Jeannie agonized for twenty years trying to have a baby. She envisioned having a little girl she could dress in cowboy boots and overalls. She ached to hold a child in her arms and sing lullabies and tell bedtime stories to. She fantasized about ribbons and bows in her little girl's long wavy hair.

Two months before her fortieth birthday my sister gave birth to a beautiful three pound five ounce baby girl. The child had to be taken early to preserve my sister's life. Pre-eclampsia was forcing the doctors to take the baby at only twenty-nine weeks gestation. She was tiny, but she was healthy.

At the age of three years old, she weighed seventeen pounds. She had long blonde hair that made her look like a little doll. The day she cut her hair my sister cried. Selena had found the scissors and did a ponytail ectomy. I asked Selena when she was six if she would ever cut her hair again. She said, "No, cause that makes my Momma cry."

Branded!!

*A*nyone who thinks sisters don't fight has never met up with mine. I was a Lily-livered coward. I would rather hide than face my foe.

Jeannie was the swordsman. She would get anything with a long handle and joust her way to victory. Lois was the tormentor. She liked to hurt and maim. Most of our battles took place while our parents were away.

One such time Lois must have run out of ideas of how to torture me into doing her part of the assigned chores. Momma always said before she left us at home together, "I want this mess cleaned up by the time I get home. If it's not done, all three of you will get a whipping."

Jeannie divided up the chores. I was never satisfied with the load I was saddled with. I hated housework. I still do.

Often I would shirk my portion of the work until Lois or Jeannie would do it to spare their own hides. Lois cured me of this one day by heating a butcher knife on the gas cook stove and branding me on the leg with it. Momma's reaction was, and I quote, "If you would do what I asked you to do she would not have done that."

The Puppy Nest

*O*ur sweet old momma dog was about to give birth to her seventh or eighth litter of mixed breed puppies.

We could only estimate her due date as we had no idea when she conceived. She was quite large in her own right, but she was becoming grotesque in her girth as the day approached for her to bless us with her final 'tour' of motherhood. She whelped nine beautiful pups one day while we were in church.

Daddy did not want her to deliver under the house again so he closed off the crawl space entrance. He did not want the pups in the garage either.

The old dog must have searched everywhere before deciding where to welcome her brood into the world. She had those puppies in an abandoned hen's nest. When she showed up at the back door looking skinny and with teats drooping to the ground we went on a puppy safari.

Lois found them in the nest and exclaimed loudly. "Look everybody, Sandy laid some puppies!"

Walk on the White Part

*W*hen my baby sister was still just a toddler, I would walk to the nearby grocery store with her. Sometimes I took her with me when I went uptown to the library. The trip to the library required a forty-five minute bus ride. Often I would carry her, but sometimes I allowed her to walk.

She was a stout child and carrying her became a burden. Of course, she had to walk when I had groceries to carry. I let her carry the bread so she would feel a sense of usefulness. I made her walk on the skirt of the curb with myself on the outside next to any possible traffic. Our neighborhood was now blessed with sidewalks.

Myra learned at an early age to look both ways before crossing a street and to always walk facing the traffic.

Years later when she walked to school she still felt safe because she always walked on the white part. She informed me not too long ago that she taught her own kids to do the same thing when they were little.

The Bowling Tournament

My future husband was dating my older sister at the time. It was one of the many times we had gone home with him between church services. This particular Sunday afternoon, we decided to go bowling. Jeannie and I had never been bowling in our lives. Neither of us had an inkling of an idea of how to choose a ball, score points and most of all the rules of etiquette such as lane usage r distracting other bowlers.

Don was a gentleman in every sense of the word. He was not a very good bowler himself, but we made him look good. He had to work harder to lose to us, than he ever had to win. He was the only one who knew how to keep score so he made up his own scoring system to make sure me and my sister would win. He did some creative scoring and some awesome fumbles to avoid making any strikes or spares.

He demonstrated time and time again how to send the ball into the gutter at the last possible moment. He even went so far as to "accidentally' jump the gutter in our lane and knock down three pins in the next lane.

I topped that when I sent my ball hurling toward the far end of the lane with the pinsetter guard still down.

Don shrieked and lunged for my ball swatting it to the left gutter about half way to the impending disaster.

I won the tournament with thirty-two points. That was thirty-two points in thirty frames of sheer torture. Now I know who killed chivalry.

Singing Down The Rain Barrel

The kids who lived behind the church we attended in our early childhood to young adulthood used to invite us to come play in their yard on Wednesday evenings while our parents were in prayer meeting. We enjoyed the swing, the homemade see-saw, and telling ghost stories and jokes.

They had a fifty[five gallon barrel partially sunk in the back yard in which they collected rainwater for washing clothes. When the barrel was only partly full ones voice would echo nicely. The only problem was, we had to get down on all fours to get our heads in sufficiently to produce a resonant tone that was the least bit melodic.

All the kids told me if I put my head into the first ring and sang into the barrel, it would sound really good. I was short so I had to get into a very awkward position to accomplish this. I had my head in the barrel. I was on my knees with my rear end in the air. I sang one of my favorite songs. When I raise up, expecting to hear applause, there was no one around. They had left me all alone in the most embarrassing physical position doing the dumbest thing and got a camera and took my picture.

I think what I once heard is true; the stupidity it took to do the thing you just did is directly proportionate to the number of people who saw you do it.

The Fox Trap

*O*ur friend Charlie Hodges, his sister Janet, and brother Gary were having a problem with a fox that kept robbing the eggs from the henhouse. Charlie got the big old animal trap from the shed and decided to teach that old fox a lesson.

We just happened to be visiting their country homestead one evening when a clamor came from the henhouse and chickens scattered everywhere only an hour or so after sundown. It was almost dark, when the fox saw the flashlight approaching, he ran back into the woods.

Charlie put his foot on the trap and Gary spread the jaws, but as soon as they let go, it sprang shut. Charlie was trying his best to appear manly and in control, but the trap was too rusty and too strong for him to handle.

After what seemed like forever, Janette offered, "Here Charlie, you hold the light and I'll set the trap." Janette was all of four years old and forty pounds soaking wet.

Bipbommas

*O*ur family had strange nicknames for everyday items. They referred to underwear as Bipbommas.

Momma had only five pair which she had washed and hung on the outdoor clothes line. She always hung the four freshly washed panties side by side on the line.

One day we were in an unfamiliar neighborhood, looking for the new home of some friends of my parents. We were looking for anything we might recognize as theirs to help us find them.

There was a house with a clothesline full of laundry hanging on it. Several sizes were noticed. This could be the house we were looking for.

My sister, Lois was only three but she was helping us try to find the correct address.

Lois looked at the clothesline and began to count, "One, two, three, four, five, Oh, shammy, shammy, that lady don't got no bipbommas on!"

Lois informed the lady of that fact when we went inside that house to visit Momma and Daddy's friends.

To Heck With Hector

My husband and I went with my sister to the lake where my parents lived. We had no luck with rod and reel, but we did catch a small catfish with our hands We decided to take it home and make a pet out of it.

We named him Hector. We put him in a mason jar to take him home, stopping on the way to buy a fish tank.

We got home and set up Hector's new home. He seemed quite content. We felt he might be a little lonely so we went and bought some tropical fish to keep him company.

We set up the heater for the fish and gradually introduced them to the tank. We had aerators, gravel, decorations, and seaweed, all for their enjoyment.

The next morning, all the fish we had bought were making themselves at home but Hector was belly-up. We had accidentally cooked him!

We enjoyed the rest of the tropical fish for a long time. Hector was the start of a fish avalanche. We increased the tank size three times before we were able to make ourselves give up our fish ranch. That was one very expensive 'free' fish.

Christmas 1951

$\mathcal{A}$ll I wanted for Christmas was a swing set. I was not interested in dolls, clothes or any other toys. I only wanted a swing set.

We lived in a big drafty old house on St. Louis Street. In Fort Worth across from the rail road tracks.

Momma put the tree up in the front window and decorated the porch with lights. Come Christmas morning I was the first one up and at the tree. We opened the gifts from Aunt Jo and Grandma and our parents.

I was growing more and more disappointed as I began to realize that the swing set was not in any of the packages under that tree. It was not even in the biggest box.

The cold air outside and the cool air inside, caused the windows of that old house to frost, making it impossible to see through.

Momma picked me up into her lap and wiped away the frost on the kitchen window. There in the backyard was my swing set.

The Clay Chicken

*E*very so often during our childhood, my sister or I would get a box of colored modeling clay.

We became experts at creating clay worms. That seemed to be the extent of our talent in our pre-school days.

Soon, we discovered, if we made a ball and pinched up a small amount of clay on one side and a larger amount on the opposite side, one could create what appeared to be a chicken.

With lots of practice, the balls of clay began to resemble a fairly decent laying hen. We fashioned a nest by rolling the clay as thin as possible, before coiling it. We were careful to make the nest the perfect size for our hens.

I remember playing a trick on Rita Fay Lunsford when she was only three and not yet developed in her cognitive skills. We made our hens and nests. We showed them to her. We removed the hen from the nest so she could see that it was two parts. We then told her to go away, we called her back in just a few seconds. Low and behold, the hens had laid eggs.

We repeated this time and again to her delighted and amazement. As a five-year-old, I can be made to believe a clay chicken can lay clay eggs.

A Cookie For Corrie

My sister Myra, left her three youngest children in the care of their grandfather to take the two older children to get school clothes. The twins were age four and their sister was about eighteen months old at the time.

Pawpaw was at the kitchen table, while the kids played in the other part of the house. Pawpaw called out to the kids, "Who wants a cookie?" This query brought the twin boys running in a flash. When Corrie did not present herself, Pawpaw inquired, "Where's Corrie?" "She's in there," was the boys' reply while pointing to the utility room. Pawpaw got up to see what was detaining the child. Seeing no one, he asked the boys again, 'Where's Corrie?"

Having followed their Pawpaw to the doorway of the utility room, they indicated she was in the freezer. My Daddy opened he upright freezer to see his granddaughter smiling. It seemed the kids were playing a game they called 'Milk jug.' and it was Corrie's turn to be the milk. There was no way of knowing how long she had been in that freezer.

If Daddy hadn't offered a cookie, if the boys had tired of the game, if, if, if.

The very next day, Daddy put a hasp and pad lock on the freezer door.

Granny's Biscuits

$\mathcal{A}$ dear friend of ours who passed away only a few years ago, was Pastor's mother, who everyone called "Granny." She was loved by many, but I loved her like she was my real Granny, as my grandparents had died while I was still in my twenties.

One time granny went to the supermarket to buy a large amount of groceries. As she was unloading the bags from her car's back floorboard, unknown to granny a cylinder of biscuits rolled under the front seat.

It was a typically hot day in East Texas. The biscuits got warm and just as Granny got back into her car to go on the next leg of her errands, the can of biscuits exploded.

Granny thought the car had blown up. It scared her half to death. After she settled a bit, she began picking biscuit dough out of the springs under the front seat of her car. It was a mess, but she was so relieved to know, what really happened, she laughed out loud. Granny always believed in praising God that the bad things weren't worse.

Peel and Pop

My sister Lois, had finally reached the magical age of potty training. Our grandfather, who we called "Daddy Jim," was a carpenter, so he was able to make a big box with a hinged lid, upholstered in red vinyl to store our toys. However, Momma decided it would be best used as a panty box.

She placed it outside of the bathroom door and loaded it with underwear for three little girls. We all wore the same size back then. We were told to grab a pair of panties on the way in the bathroom to take a bath. It was also convenient for Momma to grab a pair when Lois had an accident.

Lois did something for which she would later receive a spanking. I believe it was talking in church, (she was bad about that).

When we got home she ran into the bathroom. When she came out to face the music, Daddy popped her with his hand on her backside. Pooph, was the sound the impact made. It sounded like someone fluffing a pillow.

Daddy examined the area to see what had happened. He discovered, Lois had donned extra panties to soften the effects of the blow.

Daddy popped and peeled, peeled and popped, 17 pairs of panties from my 2 year old sister's behind.

On The Ground

$\mathcal{I}$ has long been established that I am terrified of falling. I prefer to keep both feet planted firmly on the ground. It is for this reason I will not stand on a chair, table, box or even venture higher than the second rung of a well-constructed ladder.

Even as a child I was not one to enjoy being picked up and swung around by my grandfather. Although he never dropped either of my sisters. I was sure I would be his first casualty.

When I was eleven years old, my parents allowed my older sister and I to spend a week with our Aunt and Uncle in Warr Acres, Oklahoma. Their boys were about five and six but already they were riding bikes and roller skating like champions.

My sister and I had never been on skates in our lives. It was an exciting challenge for her, but it was a nerve shattering experience for me. I bravely allowed the attendant of the roller rink to lace my rented skates. I sat for an hour or more trying to find the courage just to stand up.

I shuffled my feet on the floor under the table where I sat sipping soda pop. When the urge to visit the ladies room hit me, I was horrified! What was I to do? Should I take the skates off? Should I try to skate to the restroom? Should I ask for help? Finally, I got up and hugging the chicken rail, I slowly skated to the necessary destination.

While I was in the restroom the rink programmer announced 'snake dance." All the skaters would hold hands in a long line and skate in a snake-like fashion around the roller rink. The faster the music played the faster the skaters would go. They whipped around the rink grabbing the hands of idle skaters as they passed. Just as I stepped out of the restroom on my tip toes and made it over to the rink floor to grab the security rail, I was snatched by the kid at the end of the snake. That was the most terrifying two minutes of my life! I know I was screaming but the music was so loud no one heard me. I was glad I had already relieved myself, or I surely would have marked my trail.

Ants and Knuckles

My baby sister Myra was only four when she was made Aunt Myra by my sister, Lois.

All the time Lois was pregnant we felt it was best not to make too much ado about it. Lois was still quite young and had married quite suddenly. Not any more suddenly than I but for different reasons.

After Lois' daughter was born she brought the new baby to my parents' house to show her to Myra. Lois said, "Myra, this is your niece, Lori Lynne. You are an Aunt."

To this Myra replied, "and you are an old beetle bug. It was a difficult task to explain to that child what an Aunt was.

Even more difficult was explaining what an Uncle was. She could not grasp the difference between ants and Aunt and Uncles and knuckles. All she knew was she was not a bug and forget about explaining why this little baby was so nice.

Gary's Favorite Song

*W*hen Jeannie and I were adolescents we attended Sunday School every week at Bible Baptist Church in Kennedale, Texas. Our teacher was a lady by the name of Gertrude Grammer. There were about sixteen kids regular attendance. The Lunsford girls and Richardson girls and boy.

The Kelly's two middle kids and the Neal family's three eldest, to name just a few. One of the loners besides my future life-mate was Gary Hammond. He was later adopted by our Pastor when he was 14 years old after his parents died .

Mrs. Grammer always let us take turns choosing the song we sung at the close of the Sunday School hour. We all had our favorite song, I suppose. I liked to sing 'Jacob's ladder' Jeannie liked 'Do Lord. Other's liked, '*I'm in the Lord's Army* or '*Jesus loves me.*'

Gary's favorite song, however was one that had no biblical foundation. Each time it was his turn to choose the song we knew we

would be singing *The Ants Go Marching.*
All ten verses with animation.

The Ants go marching one by one,
hurrah, hurrah!

Miracles Or Coincidence

My Uncle, who lived in California passed away rather unexpectedly. Our family was financially unprepared for a trip to such a faraway place, as we lived in Texas.

We had an old 1946 Pontiac that Daddy felt would make the trip. He loaded up the truck with all the necessities and off we went from Fort Worth to San Francisco. It was a grueling trip across four states. It is four if you consider the number of miles to the Texas-New Mexico lines.

We only had enough money for gasoline. Daddy was between paychecks so he borrowed money from Grandma. He hoped we could make the trip on forty dollars. Gasoline was 29 cents a gallon. By taking food with us, we were sure we would do fine barring any setbacks.

Wc had bologna and bread and lots of cookies grandma had made for our trip plus a large ice chest for a milk jug of tea and a case of soft drinks. We also had a water jug and some bananas.

Momma and Daddy decided it would be best to leave the baby with Grandma so they would not have to bring the house as is so often with the case of newborns, they need everything. Lois was only four months old and they knew she would be difficult and make the trip harder for them to handle.

We were well on our way when something went wrong with the car. The engine began to overheat. We were in the desert and there was no water for miles. The heat became overwhelming and my sister got a horrible nosebleed.

We sat in the car while the heat from the noonday desert felt like it was just over our heads. Daddy was trying very hard to stop the gush of blood from my sister's nose. An ice truck passed us. The driver must have sensed we were in trouble because he turned around and came back to us. The man put a fifty pound block of ice on the steaming hood of our car and said he would send help. He shook my dad's hand and left. Daddy took out his pocket knife and chipped off a handful of ice. Wrapping the ice in his handkerchief, he place it on my sister's nose and the bleeding gradually slowed until it stopped completely.

Soon the engine was sufficiently cooled and we were able to continue our journey.

Somehow in all the excitement and panic the loaf of bread got trampled and was no longer edible. We were all hungry and we needed bread to make bologna sandwiches. My sisters and I made our discontent known (which is not unusual) when empty tummies overrule our desire to obey my parents and be quiet.

Suddenly, we noticed in the roadway ahead there was a flock of birds swooping down to get something, and then flying off in all directions. As we got closer, we could see, the birds were collecting slices of bread from the road.

As we drove further still, we could see another fowl family fighting over the spoils of three more loaves of bread.

I know we must have all prayed silently because a few miles down the lonesome desert highway, was a bread truck pulled over to the side of the rode. The driver was closing the rear doors of the truck. We all shouted as we passed him by, Thank you!! We thanked God too!

Little stories like this, serve to make a person who they are. This one is me.

//The End//